How Capitalism Ends

History, Ideology and Progress

How Capitalism Ends

History, Ideology and Progress

Steve Paxton

Winchester, UK
Washington, USA

JOHN HUNT PUBLISHING

First published by Zero Books, 2023
Zero Books is an imprint of John Hunt Publishing Ltd., No. 3 East St., Alresford,
Hampshire SO24 9EE, UK
office@jhpbooks.com
www.johnhuntpublishing.com
www.zero-books.net

For distributor details and how to order please visit the 'Ordering' section on our website.

ISBN: 978 1 80341 000 5
978 1 80341 001 2 (ebook)
Library of Congress Control Number: 2022931596

A CIP catalogue record for this book is available from the British Library.

Design: Matthew Greenfield

UK: Printed and bound by CPI Group (UK) Ltd, Croydon, CR0 4YY
Printed in North America by CPI GPS partners

Contents

Endorsements for Steve Paxton's earlier works

Steve Paxton brings a rare clarity of critical perspective to the complexities of Soviet History.
Geoff Eley, Professor of Contemporary History, University of Michigan.

Steve Paxton's timely book reclaims a vital part of humanity's conceptual toolbox, just as we witness the persisting dry cough of capitalism approach its distressing conclusion. Highly recommended
Alan Moore, author of *Watchmen, V for Vendetta* and *Jerusalem*.

Introduction

In 2009 Mark Fisher suggested that it's 'easier to imagine the end of the world than the end of capitalism' and he was probably right.[1] Imagining the end of the world requires us only to conceive of the absence of everything we know. Imagining the end of capitalism requires us to come up with some ideas about what might replace it, and about how we might get from here to there. With almost 50 percent of the world's population living in poverty and 9 million people a year dying for want of food, we'd better hope this isn't as good as it gets.[2]

If we want to understand how capitalism ends, then we need to understand what capitalism is and how it arose. We might then be in a position to know whether it's possible to move on – and if so then how, and to what? We also need to understand the nature of historical progress and the ways in which large-scale, lasting changes are driven by a dynamic interaction between technological developments and human rationality. This is the process which saw capitalism emerge from the feudal past, and it's the process which will see us move forward, away from capitalism into something else. I'll argue that a post-capitalist future which lies broadly within the concept of socialism is both desirable and obtainable.

I'll spend some time here discussing the shortcomings of the capitalist economic structure and the inconsistencies of capitalist ideology, but it's important to avoid a one-dimensional approach in which everything about capitalism is undesirable, and everything undesirable is so because it's capitalist. Capitalism is a specific historical phenomenon and, for all its ills, it has delivered significant advances over pre-capitalist societies for people in a vast range of economic and social circumstances.

While there has always been a terrible human cost to capitalist development, there was also a rationale – increased productive capacity raised living standards and life expectancy for huge swathes of the world's population. Complaints against capitalism's injustices have long been met with references to its efficiency – the pie may not be evenly divided, but it relentlessly increases in size. It's worth asking, though, whether more productive capacity is always what we need from our economic system. At some point there will be sufficient capacity and a system geared to always producing more at the expense of any other goal will cease to be the optimum system for our needs.[3] Perhaps it's also, now, worth asking if that point has already arrived – or if it's imminent. Although millions die for want of food every year and billions more are malnourished, it's not because we lack the resources to stop that from happening – globally we throw away 28 percent of the food we produce[4] and on average citizens in OECD countries produce 2 kilos of waste every single day.[5] In the heyday of capitalism firms built their reputations on reliable, long-lasting products. Reliability and longevity are product characteristics which in some sectors are no longer profitable – they can put companies out of business in today's consumer markets. Through built-in obsolescence and other aspects of disposable consumerism we are manufacturing demand in many instances, not meeting it – and this has serious and detrimental effects on us as people, on our societies and on our environment.

The major problems we face in the twenty-first century are not caused by insufficient productive capacity, but by the absence of mechanisms in place to distribute the fruits of that capacity more reasonably. Currently 26 billionaires have the same wealth as the poorest three and a half billion people on the planet – and almost all of those three and a half billion live in poverty – with limited access to food, clean water, basic medicines, shelter, security and education.[6] Is it possible for these absurdities to be solved within a capitalist economic structure, or must we find a way to progress beyond capitalism in order to overcome these issues?[7] The idea that capitalism can be reformed so that these problems can be addressed within its parameters takes something of a blow when we find, for example – as we will in Chapter 7 – Jerome Powell, Chairman of the US Federal Reserve, arguing that sometimes interest rates must be changed because otherwise *not enough Americans will be living in poverty*.[8] If those charged with fine-tuning the economy for maximum performance consider insufficient poverty to be a situation that needs addressing, it does look like we're going to need to move on to something else...

This iniquitous distribution of resources under capitalism is matched by an absurd approach to the distribution of effort. Capitalism's unprecedented capacity to advance productive technology has continually provided the means to produce goods with less effort than was previously required. But the benefits of such developments cannot be shared widely under a capitalist system and, typically, advances in productive technology push huge numbers of workers into unemployment. Surely one of the most absurd elements of technological development under capitalism is that those whose lives are blighted by drudgery and toil have learnt to fear the invention of any machine that might decrease the amount of drudgery and toil they're required to endure. The solutions currently on offer for such needless suffering range from the dismissive to the inane. In Chapter 3 we'll find Barack Obama (one of the more progressive voices in the capitalist camp) defending pointless employment on the grounds that some employment is better than no employment, even if the work being done is not work that needs doing (and even though there is valuable work that needs doing, that isn't getting done!).[9] We'll cover the details in Chapter 3, but essentially he was asserting that a solution which would be more efficient and require less paperwork couldn't be adopted for the specific reason that it would be more efficient and require less paperwork. Could it be that the market isn't the infallible, value-maximising mechanism that some seem to think?

It's one thing to assert that capitalism has passed its use-by date, and that what we need now is something different, but it's another to work out what that something is and how we might get from here to there. It's in answering this question that we'll lean heavily on an analytical approach to transformative change, informed by an understanding of historical examples of such transformations.

This work is presented in three parts – History, Ideology and Progress. The fullest appreciation of my position will be gained by approaching the chapters in the order in which they're presented, but the later chapters should still make sense in isolation, and if readers prefer to dive straight into the ideological debates of Part II – or even to discover the proposals for our future direction in Part III – then that should not pose a problem (though such readers may occasionally need to refer back to earlier chapters to arm themselves with the full context of the arguments).

Part I—History

This section aims to understand where we are today and how we got here – not only in terms of the particular events that make up our back-story, but in terms of understanding how historical change happens and its relationship to progress. Chapter 1 reviews our current predicament and establishes a definition of capitalism with reference to its essential features – structural characteristics which meaningfully set it apart from the pre-capitalist world. Here, we'll also outline an approach to understanding the mechanisms of historical change. If we want to know what the transition out of capitalism might look like, then perhaps an understanding of the processes by which it arose is a reasonable place to start. We're not so much looking for a checklist of symptoms of change here, but trying to gain some historical perspective. How does technological development interact with rationality and ideology? What kinds of material changes accompany or produce shifts in the way we understand the world and our place in it? In Chapter 2 we'll look at the emergence of capitalism in early-modern England, then briefly in France and the US, and finally at the processes leading to the establishment of capitalism in Russia. In Chapter 3 we'll review the current state of capitalism and ask whether it has become untenable. Throughout this section we'll be asking what change looks like and how it comes about. What is a revolution? Is it the same as an uprising? Must heads roll? Can significant change happen gradually? How do the personal decisions of individuals aggregate across a society and add up to social transformation? Why were turnips and sheep manure more important than Cromwell or Robespierre in the emergence of capitalism?

Part II— Ideology

In Part II, we move on to consider the ideology of the capitalist era – even if capitalism is experiencing material difficulties, or it fosters gross inequalities and is unreformable in that respect, its supporters will argue that it remains the only ethical system, as (they claim) it delivers freedoms which other systems cannot. We find, though, that – in crucial respects – the philosophical basis of capitalism is no less absurd than its mechanisms for the distribution of resources and effort we noted above. Chapter 4 reviews the political landscape of the capitalist era through an examination of the concept of the left-right spectrum. Taking account of historical context as well as contemporary politics, we find that a dynamic view of the concepts of *left* and *right* and their evolution allows us to resolve many of the difficulties surrounding the terms. This analysis gives us a new perspective on contemporary issues. On the left it gives context to debates between liberals and socialists on issues such as identity politics and class reductionism. On the right it helps to explain what the Trump(ism)-Johnson-Brexit landscape means and the direction of this 'new conservative' right.[10]

In Chapter 5 (*Equality of What?*) we ask what ought to be the currency of egalitarian justice. The emergence of capitalism was accompanied and legitimised by a philosophical opposition to feudal hierarchies which had been stifling capitalist development. Doctrines of *Divine Right* and the *Great Chain of Being* were supplanted by the Enlightenment ideals of equality encapsulated in the US *Declaration of Independence* (1776) and the French *Declaration of the Rights of Man and the Citizen* (1789). Although the equality demanded by capitalist philosophy is strictly limited to equality before the law and (eventually) equality of political participation, and although *really-existing capitalism* has often failed to deliver even on these limited ideals, it's important to note that the ideology of the capitalist era does insist on equality of *something*. From this historical context we can begin to build a picture of some degree of ideological continuity between capitalism and socialism. Each constitutes a consecutive phase in the Enlightenment project – in the transition from religion and tradition to rationality and modernity.

The decisive and instrumental ideological difference between capitalism and socialism is the relationship between the two concepts at the centre of the discussion in Chapter 6 – *Property and Freedom*. As we'll see, the capitalist conception of this relationship is beset with inconsistencies – it requires the word freedom to mean different things at different points in the argument – and sometimes it has to mean something that no one really thinks is what 'freedom' means. We'll also look at the claim that the *right to own property* is an absolute requirement of freedom, and how that sits with the capitalist insistence that *not actually owning any property* doesn't infringe or even slightly diminish anyone's freedom. We'll trace the development of this ideological sleight of hand from John Locke to Robert Nozick and beyond, taking in the Putney Debates in the aftermath of the first English Civil War and the ideological context of the French Revolution as well as contributions from Hayek, Berlin, Rawls, Frankfurt and others along the way.

Part III— Progress

Having determined that capitalism is both materially outmoded and ideologically defunct we move on in Part III to investigate ways in which we might best manage the transition out of capitalism and discuss potential policies to ensure we move in the right direction, so that its successor is a more just and civilised economic structure. In Chapter 7 we'll look at some of the social and cultural changes we'll need to prepare for, particularly with regard to our conception of the role of work in our lives and to the relationships between work and reward in society. Chapter 8 examines the insights which Modern Monetary Theory brings to bear on the operations of the economy in late-stage capitalism, as well as Thomas Piketty's proposals which, although from a more orthodox economic perspective, are more radical in substance than the policy positions often derived from an MMT approach.[11] In Chapter 9 we'll discuss some examples of policies which aim to really drive us past the capitalist economic structure and how they might be implemented.

It's impossible for any reasonably informed person to think about how humankind might approach the future without taking account of the climate emergency we currently face. I have not addressed the details of *how* we might tackle this emergency here – there are many others far better qualified to undertake that task. It should, though, be clear from the arguments I present – and in case it isn't, I'll state it explicitly now – that the climate emergency cannot be adequately addressed while it is a subordinate consideration to the pursuit of profit and the (illogical) capitalist conception of freedom. We need to move politically, socially and economically beyond those constraints in order to address the impending environmental disaster, and the aim of this work is to examine how we might do so. That is not to say, of course, that there is no point doing all we can for the planet in the meantime – it's merely the acknowledgement that a system that cannot survive without growth is incompatible with the survival of the planet. We need a *Green New Deal*. This book addresses the *New Deal* part of that approach, but that should not be taken as any kind of signal that the *Green* part is not paramount. (Or, for that matter, that the *New Deal* part, like the programme from which it takes its name, can be carried out within the confines of the existing system. We are past that point.)

The themes we'll return to throughout the book revolve around the question of how change happens and the interaction between technological progress and human rationality. Capitalism is viewed as a historical phenomenon which emerged despite no one planning or even really envisioning it. Certain conditions existed in which it made rational sense for certain people to act in certain ways – the upshot of all this was, eventually, the emergence of a capitalist economic structure. The success of capitalism has rendered those conditions obsolete and the way forward now is to encourage the conditions in which it makes rational sense to enough people to make the decisions which will amount to us progressing to something better. Part of that process will be provided by technological advances – the rest will be up to us. We need to ensure we respond appropriately to those advances, and this work aims to contribute to the conversation about what our responses should look like.

Part I
History

1

Capitalism and Progress

And yet, something has changed for the better. We have rediscovered that capitalism is not the answer, but the question
Eric Hobsbawm, 2012[12]

The aim of this section is to understand capitalism from a world historical perspective – how it emerged, how it's developed and where it might be heading. Essential to this process are a clear definition of what capitalism is and an approach to understanding the processes of historical change. This first chapter begins with a brief summary of our current situation and then places the turmoil in a longer-term perspective.

1.1 Where We Are Now

Even before any of us had heard of Covid-19 our news agenda was already dominated by alarming events – Brexit, Trump, Putin, Johnson and the rise of the far right in Hungary, Brazil and elsewhere. The failures of the Johnson and Trump administrations to deal with the pandemic with any kind of wisdom or competency have not surprised any reasonably informed observers on either side of the Atlantic. Both men are widely regarded as dishonest and corrupt[13] but the extent of the assaults on their respective constitutions and on the institutions of liberal democracy in both countries have shocked and disorientated onlookers from across the political spectrum.[14]

In the US and the UK, it's now commonplace to observe that actual events are so absurd as to be impossible to satirise. At the same time, the increase in politically motivated public violence and abuse, including the assassination of British MP Jo Cox and credible death threats to other Labour MPs, the resurgence of the far right in several countries and the normalisation of dangerous propaganda in response to the pandemic have seen confusion replaced by fear and panic. When the New British Union of Fascists turn up at a rally in Trafalgar Square and are not even the most worrying or dangerous people in attendance, there is justifiable concern that the scarcely credible events unfolding on the nightly news are symptoms of impending chaos – that as a society we are regressing under the spell of populist dogma. And yet...

And yet on the whole, despite the legacy of Thatcher and Reagan, despite the rise of Putin, despite Brexit, Johnson and Trump, it's not the case that there is *nothing* to celebrate in the world. Global poverty rates continue to decrease (though less quickly than in earlier decades). For the first time ever, on average, girls receive almost as much education as boys. Child mortality has plummeted, smallpox has been eradicated, cancer survival rates improve all the time, HIV is survivable. Global average life expectancy has risen from 26 in 1820 to 73 today. In 1900 a fifth of new-borns died before their first birthday – the figure is now around 1 per cent.[15] Every day across the world millions of people, in all kinds of situations, at all levels of income and ability, work to improve the human condition and the lives of those most in need. The society we have built is capable of brilliant and hugely complex humanitarian achievements. While the news headlines can be alarming, the background against which they're presented includes many long-term achievements – and although such improvements have been disproportionately beneficial to those of us in the 'developed world', many of the benefits have been seen globally.

How are we to reconcile these conflicting currents? How can we explain the prevailing political climate in the UK and the US[16], and the resurgence of the far right elsewhere, against this backdrop of progress and achievement? I will argue that while we are indeed entering a period of significant historical change, the rumblings of right-wing populism, in the UK and

US, Brazil, Hungary and elsewhere, represent symptoms of change, but not bellwethers for the direction of that change. They are the death agony of the old structure, not a dawn chorus of the new. Times of structural change will always cause some discomfort for those who had internalised the worldview which legitimised the political, social and cultural relations that served the economic structure now under stress. It's not always easy to accept that deeply-felt convictions have become outdated – to unlearn a world view that has permeated society for generations. In the UK and the US, the populist media – and populist politicians – have for decades nurtured a backwards-looking political culture, fixated on past glories and wary of change. Until recently, this undercurrent had been largely reduced to relatively benign levels – focusing in the UK, for example, on the pomp and circumstance of the monarchy, unrealistic ambitions for the English national football team[17]and a much higher opinion of Churchill than that which led the wartime generation to reject the Conservative Party under his leadership at every opportunity.[18] Since the referendum on EU membership in 2016, though, the sinister edge to this backward-looking world view has again reared its head, as its high profile advocates manoeuvre their 'culture war' into the forefront of political debate.

Parallel to – and overlapping with – this cultural arena, other dimensions of social, economic and political discourse have become similarly polarised, with Jeremy Corbyn and Bernie Sanders pulling discourse to the left and Boris Johnson and Donald Trump dragging their followers further to the right even than Thatcher and Reagan had managed in the 1980s.[19] While polarisation in itself isn't necessarily a problem, when it's combined with an increasingly superficial discourse – encouraged by the nature of social media – it contributes to a process of lowering the quality of public debate. As a part of this process, it has become almost impossible to conduct a nuanced conversation about the nature of capitalism – for some it's responsible for every ill on the planet, for others it's the saviour of mankind. I'm not going to referee that debate. I'm going to tell you it's the wrong debate. Capitalism is here whether we like it or not. And it's going away too, whether we like *that* or not. Much though some of capitalism's least convincing advocates like to portray it as some kind of natural order, or the inevitable, default condition of human society, it is in the end no more eternal than the Roman Empire or the Kingdom of Aksum[20] or Real Madrid's domination of the European Cup.

1.2 How We Arrived Here

In considering if and how capitalism might be replaced, it's useful to understand what kind of processes are likely to constitute a transformation from one economic structure to another, and a good starting point for that project is to look at the means by which capitalism itself developed out of European feudalism. There are numerous approaches to understanding the origins and development of capitalism and I'll focus on one that provides a strong analytical framework from which to understand historical change. One of the central claims arising out of this framework is that capitalism is the only economic system capable of delivering the rapid technological development and material abundance of the last 200 years. This claim is a stalwart of the advocates of capitalism, and is often employed as a justification for capitalism's continued existence for all eternity. But one of the earliest proponents of the claim – for whose theory this was an absolutely central tenet – saw in it the seeds of capitalism's eventual expiry. It comes as a surprise to many who revel in capitalism's unique and seemingly boundless capacity for growth that the first economist to build his theory of historical development around this capacity was Karl Marx. (Don't panic, read on…)

Although Marx provides us with some useful insights into

the process of historical change, my aim here is not to evaluate the pros and cons of his work as a whole, but to use some of the explanatory tools and conceptual categories he devised and developed, with the aim of making sense of the past as more than a random collection of dates and events. Marx's economics and politics are not central to this process, but his theory of history – often referred to as *historical materialism* – will provide a scaffolding to assist us in building a picture of where we are, how we got here and where we're going. Although Marx is regularly misrepresented by the right, the breadth of his work is also somewhat under-represented by the left. That's not to say that the ideas with which many of us are familiar have been dishonestly attributed to Marx by those on the left. Rather, the events of the twentieth century, and the work of some of the personalities thrown into prominence by those events, have resulted in a relatively narrow understanding of the possibilities available to a historical materialist approach. The central concept of **revolution**, for example, is almost always taken to refer to a sudden, violent overthrow of political power, yet Marx writes extensively about the revolution by which capitalism superseded feudalism and describes its gradual progress over a couple of hundred years. In Chapter 2 we'll look at that revolution and note that the real drivers of the emergence of capitalism in Europe were not 'revolutionary' characters like Cromwell or Robespierre, but technological innovations and new ideas about property, freedom and individual rights. From this perspective the core process of change is the interaction between technological development and human rationality. The term *revolution* applies to a degree and type of historical change, not to the means by which it is achieved or the timescale involved. As we'll see, this also means that we need to broaden our ideas about what constitutes a 'revolutionary action'. The revolution which saw capitalism replace feudalism included actions of landlords and merchants, such as the conversion of customary rents to commercial rents and conducting trade outside of markets controlled by local boroughs. A revolution doesn't have to involve manning the barricades or storming the Winter Palace. It's entirely possible (conceptually, at least) for the revolutionary transition to occur peacefully.

There are many ways of analysing and categorising historical change, and they're not necessarily mutually exclusive. Each approach delivers its own insights and has its own limitations. Sometimes different approaches just occupy different explanatory planes. While some historians might focus on the evolution of political systems, and classify societies as empires, monarchies, democracies, dictatorships and so on, from a historical materialist perspective, the defining characteristics of societies in different stages of development are the patterns of property ownership – not only who owned what, but also what kind of things could be owned and what rights and responsibilities came with ownership. As we'll discover, many of our current ideas about property ownership were consolidated only a few hundred years ago.

When we refer to changing ideas about property ownership, we're not really concerned with the ownership of *personal* property, but with ownership of productive resources.[21] This includes the 'means of production' – tools and machinery, factories, forests, office buildings, intellectual property, algorithms and so on, but it also includes people and their labour power. (Remember that in much of human history people themselves have been included in the set of *things which can be owned)* The term '**Production Relations**' is used to denote who owns which of these productive resources. A person may own their own labour power, or some or all of someone else's labour power. Or they may own another person, or any amount and number of means of production. Production Relations describe who owns what in the production process.[22]

It's important not to get bogged down in terminology, but on the other hand it's also crucial to be clear about what is meant by certain terms – having briefly defined *production relations* and the *means of production* above I'll limit our diversion into terminology to two more short definitions: *class* and *economic structure*.

In this context, a **class** is a group of people who share the same production relations. In general conversation the term *class* has many meanings – usually quite vague, and almost always encompassing social and cultural facets. Terms such as working class and middle class are familiar to us all, but lack agreed, formal definitions. These uses of the idea of class are not wrong or invalid – they just don't play a role in historical materialist explanations of social change. It's important to note that for our purposes the term class does not equate to an occupational category (such as the familiar ABC1 schema developed by the NRS), or an income band, or any collection of lifestyle choices or cultural signifiers. Instead we'll refer to specific, named classes, each defined by its relations of production – its members' ownership or control of productive resources. Classes are important in historical materialism because they reflect people's relationship to the production process and therefore influence the way people react to advances in productive technology. But the role of class in shaping historical change doesn't have to conform to traditional ideas about class conflict and proletarian uprisings. This will become apparent as we examine the processes of historical change throughout the next few chapters. If you're feeling that this way of classifying populations in twenty-first century advanced economies is a little jaded and out of date, don't worry. In Chapter 3 we'll discover why this approach makes for a much more usable classification in describing our current situation and the potential for historical change than ideas about 'the working class', or 'blue collar workers', or the group currently a hot topic in many US debates, the 'Professional Managerial Class', or PMC.[23]

The **economic structure** is the network of production relations in a society at a given time – that is, of which classes a society is comprised. Capitalism and feudalism are examples of economic structures and we'll look at the differences between them later, but first we should consider the means by which societies progress from one economic structure to another. In historical materialism, the **revolution** is the process whereby one economic structure – one set of production relations – is replaced by another. This is a gradual and somewhat *ad hoc* process – the sudden and violent episodes often called revolutions, or coups or civil wars are the processes whereby the political world catches up with these economic transformations. As we'll see in Chapter 2 with respect to the process that saw capitalism replace feudalism in England, the real revolution – the underlying change in production relations, can take place over a few hundred years. The English Civil Wars in the middle of the seventeenth century and the coup known as the Glorious Revolution in 1688 were the upheavals whereby the capitalist class finally wrested political power from the hands of the old order – but the actual revolutionary change, the technological and economic developments – had been slowly progressing since the start of the sixteenth century.

1.3 Understanding Historical Change

The concept of revolution introduces the dimension of time and the process of social change into the equation. How such change proceeds, and how revolutionary transformations come about can be described by the *Development Thesis* and its conceptual partner the *Primacy Thesis*, as developed by G.A. Cohen in his ground-breaking and influential 1976 interpretation of historical materialism.[24] This approach is based on two assertions:

1. Humans are sufficiently intelligent to be able to improve their material situation, and sufficiently rational to be

disposed to do so, given their historical situation of scarcity, and

2. as technology develops, different types of economic organisation suit different levels of technological development. (A slave society might be suitable for building aqueducts or keeping the Picts at bay, but it's not particularly conducive to the invention of spreadsheets or the development of ABS braking systems.)

Taken together these assertions imply that:

- historical change is driven by technological development
- various economic structures will arise and persist because they promote development at the then existing level
- as technology develops, an economic structure that had previously promoted development may now hinder further development
- in such a case, the economic structure will (eventually) give way, and a new economic structure will (eventually) emerge which promotes further development. (If economic structures sometimes impede further development, and if rationality dictates that development cannot be subverted indefinitely – then economic structures must 'rise and fall...as they enable or impede that growth'.)[25]

The process of historical change in this context is similar to the evolutionary process of natural selection by chance variation. As possibilities to improve technology arise – from the wheel and the seed drill to the factory system and artificial intelligence – humans will tend to adopt those developments, and if economic and social arrangements prevent societies from doing so, then it is those arrangements which will be surrendered, not the technological advances. (In Chapter 2 we'll see how feudal (and post-feudal) economic and social conditions hampered technological progress. Eventually, the lure of technological advances (and the benefits of their adoption) proved to be greater than the attachment to traditional, feudal customs.) Sometimes a society will, for whatever reason, choose to forego technological developments in favour of retaining some traditional economic, social, cultural or religious arrangement. (Usually because the decision-making interests in such a society are doing very well under the existing situation and have no desire to rock the boat.) Such societies soon find themselves at a military or economic disadvantage against rivals who adopted the technology in question. Over time the technology spreads, either by invasion, economic dominance or capitulation of the forces of tradition in the face of reality.

Throughout history there is constant experimentation with different ways of doing things. Not just in the development of new technologies but in the field of human relations. The variation of time, place and circumstance in the human experience has led to an incalculable number of combinations of production relations. Those experiments which favour further development at a time when existing relations are proving a drag on progress confer a productive advantage on their host societies. In the almost universal human situation of scarcity, a productive advantage translates into a competitive edge and, for that society, a survival advantage. Over time, societies (or groups within societies) adopting production relations that 'work' will come to dominate their neighbours who resist such a change – a new economic structure emerges and the process of revolution is underway. The struggle may be peaceful or bloody, and the tide may ebb and flow, but in the battle between the past and the future – the future always wins in the end. This is the process that has seen us progress through history from slavery, through various forms of feudalism and into capitalism.

It's also the process that will see us progress from capitalism to something else. Capitalism, as its advocates will point out, has delivered technological advances and material abundance to previously unimaginable levels. The approach I'll adopt here asserts that this capacity is unique to capitalism and intrinsic to its nature, but also that this very aspect of the character of capitalism is its fatal flaw. In short, capitalism has developed technology to a point where it is no longer the best structure to develop technology further.[26]

1.4 What is Capitalism?

Some definitions of capitalism equate it with markets, the exchange of goods and so on – and the proponents of such definitions are thus able to claim that it's a permanent and natural feature of human existence, but such definitions are so broad as to be of no real use to anyone. Here I'll employ a definition of capitalism as an economic structure, situated historically as emerging in Western Europe over the course of the sixteenth and seventeenth centuries, and consolidating its global dominance during the nineteenth and twentieth centuries. There's no universally agreed definition of capitalism, but if you prefer an alternative to the version I propose here, that shouldn't cause us a problem – just make up a snappy name for the thing I describe and then mentally replace instances of the word 'capitalism' with your chosen descriptor for the remainder of the book. It's the concept that's important here, not the label. Note, though, that there is considerable precedent for the type of definition I'll be using. Ellen Meiskins Wood, for example, reflects a broad consensus among historians with the assertion that 'capitalism is not a natural or inevitable consequence of human nature, or of the age-old tendency to "truck, barter and exchange". It is a late and localized product of very specific historical conditions.'[27]

In defining capitalism as an economic structure, the definition will consist entirely of a description of *who owns which productive resources*, and what "ownership" means in that type of society. This focus on the character of ownership structures as the defining elements of social systems is not limited to those writing from a historical materialist perspective. Economist Thomas Piketty adopts a similar approach in his *Capital and Ideology*. Piketty refers to societies up to the present day as *inequality regimes* and classifies them by the type of wealth inequality they exhibit and the institutions and ideology which perpetuate and legitimise that inequality. The societies which I refer to as capitalist are a subset of those which he calls *proprietarian*. He reserves the term capitalism for proprietarian societies which have reached the industrial stage of technological development (though not *because* they've reached the industrial stage, but because of the necessary changes in ideas about ownership which accompany industrial development).[28] The overall approach is similar and the differences in terminology need not detain us here. The important point is that there is value in understanding historical change in the context of the way in which attitudes to property and ownership change over time, as technology develops and opens up new possibilities. (Also, as noted above, this approach need not exclude other approaches, but can complement them. When, for example, economist Robert Reich frames our predicament as a battle for democracy against oligarchy, his emphasis on political manifestations of power confronts much the same problem as our focus on property ownership, but from a different angle. It's important that we see the whole picture, rather than descending into endless nit-picking about whose theory is purest.)

Any definition of capitalism can appear abstract and irrelevant when presented in unfamiliar (and somewhat archaic) terms, but it's necessary to be clear about what we mean by the concept. A brief definition of capitalism is presented below, the value and relevance of which will become clear in later chapters.

Bear in mind that in a historical context, the chief value of a definition of capitalism is to identify what sets it apart from the economic structures which it replaced. The definition of capitalism I'll employ here is that it is an economic structure in which the dominant production relation is that most workers are proletarians. The proletariat are distinguished from pre-capitalist workers by their full ownership of their own labour power, and their non-ownership of any means of production. This is the condition of virtually all waged employees under capitalism and means that:

- they are free in that they own their own labour power and may sell it on the open market to the highest bidder – they are not compelled to work for any particular employer, but
- they are unfree in that their non-ownership of any means of production dictates that in order to live they *must* sell their labour power to some employer or other

This situation is in contrast to pre-capitalist labourers who were typically bound to the land by feudal obligations, unable to sell their labour power on the open market but compelled to labour for others, not by the need to earn their living, but by force, the threat of force or customary obligations. Workers in pre-capitalist economic structures were typically unfree in the sense that they didn't enjoy full ownership or control over their own labour power. Sometimes restrictions were formalised in their legal obligation to perform work for a feudal lord, in other cases the restrictions were less transparent, but no less real in terms of the lived experience of the worker. On the other hand, many workers enjoyed some rights over their means of subsistence: their obligations to their feudal lord may be partly reciprocated by provision of a plot of land on which they could grow crops and various rights of use or access to communal assets – the right to graze livestock on a common or to collect firewood from a spinney, for example. Capitalism sweeps away both the rights and the obligations of the feudal workers.

Under capitalism then, most people are proletarians, who own no means of production. A much smaller class are the capitalists – or bourgeoisie – who own most of the means of production. Full membership of the bourgeoisie is defined by ownership of sufficient means of production as to not need to work in order to be able to live. A bourgeois industrialist or landowner *may* actually work, but their class location requires only that they *need not* do so. These are of course ideal-typical definitions, and in capitalism, as in any system, numerous shades and intermediate classes exist. Chapter 3 includes a discussion of some intermediate classes under capitalism – chiefly technocrats and the petty-bourgeoisie – and an explanation of their potential roles in transitioning us away from the capitalist economic structure.

With these two great classes – the proletariat and the bourgeoisie – facing each other, the capitalist economic structure provides the conditions for technological development to flourish – a flexible workforce, concentrated ownership of the means of production, generous rewards for innovation and investment, production for the accumulation of capital and so on. But however perfect are these conditions for the development of technology, it is exactly that development which delivers the conditions which eventually render capitalist production relations a hindrance to further human progress.

1.5 Capitalism and Progress

As we've seen, historical materialism asserts that different economic structures *correspond* to different levels of technological development. That is to say that as technology develops, economic structures – such as feudalism and capitalism – arise when and because they promote further development at the then existing level. This formulation entails that each economic structure contains the 'seeds of its own destruction'. By facilitating and promoting further development each economic structure moves technology on to the point where the structure itself no longer corresponds to the new, higher level of development.

According to this approach, capitalism, having driven productive capacity to previously unimaginable levels, will at some point begin to hinder further progress. Here I will argue that we have reached that point. The success of capitalism – as its diehard supporters will never tire of explaining to you – lies in the ability of the *invisible hand* of the market to respond quickly and efficiently to demand.[29] If there's money to be made by satisfying a demand, some enterprising entrepreneur will satisfy that demand. Prices will settle at a point determined by exactly how much people who have money are willing to pay, ensuring that everything always sells for its exact 'value', meaning that all demands will be satisfied more 'efficiently' by the market than could ever be managed by any army of state planners. The price of anything, the number or volume required, the exact details of the product – all of these things will be determined perfectly by the market. (The limitations of this understanding, in terms of what 'value' and 'efficiently' really mean are discussed in Chapter 6.)

While the condition of the world was one of acute and generalised scarcity, capitalism's responsiveness to demand (which really means demand *combined with ability to pay*) provided innovative solutions to problems of insufficient or ineffective supply. Demand was met, problems were solved, innovations were developed, profits were made – technological progress marched on. Of course, many were left behind, but many benefitted, and in general the beneficiaries were those best placed to ensure the continuation of the system which served them well. There is no question that capitalism had its victims, and in our appreciation of history this can't be overlooked, but in our attempt to understand what capitalism is, our focus should be on the relationship between capitalism and technological development.

Up until recently, technological development tended to focus on producing more, and bigger and better. Driven by the desires of those who could back their demands with cash, capitalism ramped up this process to previously inconceivable levels. But the technological advances which have been accomplished under capitalism have created the conditions for a different paradigm and for the transition to a new economic structure. The capacity for capitalism to develop technology and for that technology to deliver material abundance means that as a global population we are no longer living in a situation of scarcity. That may seem an odd statement, given that 20,000 people still starve to death every day, but what it means is that we have eliminated scarcity in the relevant sense of it being a driver for technological progress. Capitalism drives progress by meeting demand – but only when that demand is coupled with the ability to pay. The invisible hand of the market doesn't care if people are starving – only if they're starving *and can pay for food*. This is why we end up throwing away more than a quarter of all the food we produce. In the twenty-first century, the problem of human poverty is one of distribution, not scarcity. And this situation is not confined to those literally dying for want of a more equitable distribution of produce. In the developed world inequality is increasing and bringing with it problems for people at all points on the wealth and income scale.[30]

Extensive research by Richard Wilkinson and Kate Pickett[31] has shown that quality of life across societies in the developed world – measured on any number of independently produced scales (life expectancy, infant mortality, divorce rates, suicide rates, prison population, addiction rates and many more) does not correlate at all to the overall level of wealth in a society. More importantly, though, their data also shows striking correlations between quality of life and the levels of equality in a society. More equal societies enjoy a far higher quality of life – and not just for those at the lower end of the equality spectrum. On this wide range of measures, even the richest in a relatively egalitarian society enjoy a higher quality of life than the richest in a richer, but less equal society. 'Economic growth, for so long the great engine of progress has, in the rich countries, largely finished its work. Not only have measures of wellbeing and happiness ceased to rise with economic growth but, as affluent societies have grown richer there have been long-term rises in rates of anxiety, depression and numerous other social problems.'[32]

Capitalism has delivered material abundance at a scale and pace with which no other system could compete. But scarcity is no longer our enemy, and therefore abundance is no longer our goal. Inequality, not scarcity, is what is now holding back progress to improvements in our quality of life. Equality is the new prosperity.

2

The Rise of Capitalism

Everybody was supposed to grab whatever he could and hold onto it. Some were very good at grabbing and holding, were fabulously well-to-do. Others couldn't get their hands on doodley-squat.

Kurt Vonnegut, 1973[33]

2.1 *The Development of Capitalism in England*

At the end of the seventeenth century with England's population at a little over 5 million, Geoffrey King predicted that improvements in agricultural techniques would eventually permit sufficient food production to support as many as 11 million people. He expected us to reach those giddy heights somewhere around the year 3500.[34] But King hadn't seen capitalism coming. Although by the time he was writing, many of the processes of the transition were well under way, no one could really have seen how rapidly England would change over the coming century. King's estimate of a maximum population of 11 million by 3500 was hopelessly inadequate – we passed that figure in the 1820s, and even by then we could spare over 10 per cent of our agricultural output for export.

What changed then, to enable such unimaginable growth in population? How did we suddenly manage to produce sufficient food to feed 11 million people by the 1820s, or 30 million by 1900? In order to understand what changes led to this development, we need first to understand something about pre-capitalist society.

Pre-capitalist England

At the start of the sixteenthcentury, although feudalism proper had largely disappeared its legacy was everywhere. Seventy-five per cent of the population worked on the land. Inefficient, small-scale strip farming prevailed. Production was largely for consumption and for the local market, with surpluses finding their way up the feudal hierarchy through the system of manors, and manorial lords which still dominated the countryside. These landowners – the nobility and the gentry – derived their status from customary arrangements, from the number of servants in their household and tenants bound to their land and from their proximity in the hierarchy to the monarch. Rents were usually customary, meaning that the value didn't change often or by much, and bore no relation to any market value of the property. Customary rents were symbolic representations of social hierarchies, rather than returns on investments. Rents sometimes included a money component but usually also included various labour obligations or payments in kind. Tenancies also generally included a plot of land to cultivate, as well as some rights over common assets, enabling workers to provide subsistence for themselves and their families. (In historical materialist terms, the workers enjoyed some ownership rights over some means of production.) Tenures could be for a number of years, for life, or a number of lives. Workers were not free to seek a tenancy wherever they pleased – feudal obligations tied them to their master, whose permission was required if they wished to live, work, marry or in some cases to even travel outside of their home manor. Permission, if it was granted at all, was often accompanied by a fee.

The freedom to buy and sell was limited by a maze of restrictive practices and customs. Town markets were local, and prices were fixed by the Borough. Staple produce and products were sold to individuals for personal consumption first, in fixed amounts, then to those who would use them in their trade (brewers, bakers etc), and only after this was any surplus allowed to be sold to merchants or middlemen to sell outside of the local community. Even the middlemen had to be licensed by the Borough.[35] It's not feasible to characterise the markets in either labour or commodities as 'free markets' in sixteenth-century England.

This was a system in which those working on the land enjoyed some rights of use of the land, but were also bound by custom or circumstance to their locality and their local 'social superiors'. For their part, the landowners, while rarely turning down any opportunity to increase their wealth, ran their affairs in the pursuit of status, rather than profit. This was a highly regulated and quite static society. Depending on local circumstances, change was generally either slow or non-existent. And yet change did happen – and in line with Cohen's Development Thesis, the prime mover in that process of change was technological progress.

The Agricultural Revolution

Despite the importance of figures such as Oliver Cromwell or Admiral Nelson in the public imagination, the real movers and shakers in English history were turnips and sheep manure. With 75 per cent of the working population engaged in agriculture at the start of the sixteenth century, each worker was producing enough for themselves and one-third of another person. This level of productivity is simply not enough to enable urbanisation or industrialisation on any significant scale.[36] There would need to be a revolution in agricultural production before any such progress would be possible.[37] The first stage of this process took place between 1500 and 1640.

At the start of this period, English arable farming used a three-field system of crop rotation – one field in three had to be left uncultivated each year to allow the soil to recover its nutrients, or it might be planted with legumes such as peas or beans which stimulate a process of fixing nitrates into the soil. The discovery that crops such as turnips and clover could be grown in fields normally left fallow, and greatly increase the regeneration of the soil leading to increased wheat or barley yields in subsequent years, enabled the adoption of a four-field system in which no land was left fallow.[38] The improvements to the soil led to higher wheat and barley yields, but in turnips and clover the system also provided fodder and grazing crops with which to support more livestock, which in turn increased the supply of manure for use as fertiliser, leading to even higher yields. The practice of *sheep folding* developed whereby sheep would graze during the day, and then be brought back into the fold – a moveable pen – for the night. The daytime grazing transferred nitrates from the soil into the sheep. During the night, the sheep obligingly deposited urine and manure wherever the fold had been placed, transferring the nitrates back into the soil elsewhere on the farm.[39] Farmers learnt to add lime or marl to their soil, reducing acidity and improving the conversion of organic nitrogen to mineral nitrogen which can be taken up by plants. Without any conception of the chemistry at work, a process of trial and error – and careful observation – was improving agricultural production.

As improvements in productivity began to produce a greater surplus, the more progressive landowners – perhaps those with lower status among the customary hierarchy, and therefore less to lose and more to gain, or perhaps just those of a more adventurous spirit – began to understand the potential rewards of modernising their relations with their land and with their tenants, and started to change their attitude to markets and money.[40] A market in land developed, with some landowners now viewing land as an investment opportunity rather than a status symbol. This new breed of forward-looking landowner would typically introduce modern farming techniques to their land, but would also 'modernise' their relations with their tenants. As the wool industry grew, sheep pasture became a better investment than arable land. With sheep becoming more profitable than people, progressive landowners looked for any means to free their land up for sheep pasture by displacing tenants or shifting them to a less secure or shorter-term footing.

Where possible customary rents were converted to modern market rents, copyhold to leasehold, rent-in-kind to money rents. Whereas customary rent was nominal, and remained at a fixed amount for generations, these newer 'rack rents' could be increased at will, effectively giving the landlord the power of eviction. Where conversions were not possible, copyholds were now often not renewed as they expired, leaving the tenant homeless and landless. Wastelands, woodlands and commons were enclosed, subverting common usage rights and making subsistence for the tenant farmers precarious if not impossible. As tenant farmers were squeezed off the land, their now vacant plots were added to the newly enclosed sheep pastures. Ellen Meiskins Wood summarises this process as one of 'mounting assaults on customary rights, assertions of exclusive private ownership against communal rights to common land, challenges to customary tenures and an assortment of usage rights, together with various oppressive practices and extortionate rents, accompanied by legal and theoretical efforts to redefine the meaning of property'.[41] While many landowners remained content to derive their status from a large number of socially subordinate tenants, and their income from customary rents and similar payments, the more forward-looking among them preferred the seemingly unlimited potential of market profits. A section of England's gentry were moving their operations in the direction of a more capitalist footing, and the evictions they forced on their tenants were creating a landless proletariat.

The Resistance of the Feudal State

It's important to recognise that in this period these progressive tendencies were resisted by the establishment. In 1489 and 1516, Acts were passed to limit the process of enclosure. In *Utopia* (1516) Thomas Moore criticises the enclosing landlord as an 'insatiable wretch who is a plague to his country', whose 'tenants are turned out of their possessions by tricks or by main force or by being wearied out by ill-usage'.[42] The world was changing, and those who had benefitted from the old order were mobilising the forces of tradition to resist new developments in any way they could. The crown and clergy were joined in this resistance to progress by the more traditional landowners – those benefitting most from the existing order, those who couldn't see the benefits of experimenting with new technology, the short-sighted, the risk averse, those whose religious outlook attached them to tradition, and those whose assets just didn't lend themselves to adaptation to new technologies.

Alongside the modernisation of farming methods which brought growing numbers of progressive landlords into conflict with the traditional order, the rise of a new type of merchant again reduced the income finding its way up through the system to the crown. These merchants circumvented the regulations of the guilds and the boroughs by trading in unofficial markets in unincorporated towns. Just as anti-enclosure legislation was aimed at inhibiting the activities of the modernising landowners, the traditionalists attempted to thwart the rise of the developing merchant class. Unfortunately for the crown, the chief means at its disposal was to address the apex of the merchant pyramid by increasing the use of monopolies and patents – stifling progress and innovation through a characteristically old-world system where the exclusive rights to profit from certain activities were handed out in return for loyalty. Here we see one of the first examples of the conflict between the progressive interest and the traditionalists being expressed in the struggle between Parliament and the Crown. As well as granting Sir Walter Raleigh a patent to colonise America in 1584, Elizabeth I also issued numerous other patents and monopolies – in butter, salt, beer, herrings, soap and a host of other commodities. By 1601 Parliament demanded an end to this practice by which 'a fewe were enriched and the multitude impoverished'.[43] (Note that the 'multitude' here refers to a section of the gentry, not to the great unwashed masses of seventeenth-century England.) At this point Parliament was not able to force the issue, and had to make do with half an apology and some vague promises from the Queen, but by now the writing was on the wall – the days of the old order were numbered.

Bourgeois Ascendency

With progressive farmers and merchants accumulating capital and seeking investment, with the plunder of the New World and the west coast of Africa bringing new riches and with the boom in the wool trade, greater numbers of the gentry and even the nobility started to look at the world and their place in it in a new light. The crown and its supporting structure of the traditional hierarchy saw revenues dwindle and crown finances become more stretched and therefore more reliant on raising taxes, for which they required Parliamentary consent. (In practical terms, the gentry were the only group able to enforce and collect taxes, and their interests were represented nationally by the House of Commons.)

The important thing to note is the direction of travel in this process of change. Technological developments provided a greater agricultural surplus which in turn enabled experiments with new approaches to ownership and control of the means of production. Some of these experiments enabled further developments in technology and more advances in production. The incomes of those who took up these progressive opportunities had increased, while the incomes of the traditionalists had remained static. Those who had benefitted most from the traditional hierarchy faced a choice – they could either embrace the future, or they could stick with tradition and try to cling on to the past. The crown, as the figurehead of the old order, deriving its status and legitimacy from tradition and custom, lacked the imagination to look forward to a new era and opposed innovation at every turn. As the Tudors gave way to the Stuarts the crown became even more desperate in its attempts to resist progress. The doctrine of the Divine Right of Kings was revived.[44] Parliament was suspended from 1629 until 1640 by Charles I, but reconvened when he ran out of other people's money. The political deadlock between the forces of progress, represented by Parliament, and the forces of tradition embodied in the crown was broken through 9 years of civil war and the execution of Charles I. But this struggle for political power was a symptom of the broader, longer-term economic processes described above, not the decisive train of events as portrayed in popular accounts. The crown's resistance to the way in which economic relations were changing resulted from its adherence to the social, religious and cultural capital it had invested in the system which had legitimised and facilitated its rule in earlier centuries.

The Consolidation of the Capitalist Interest

Following the victory of the modernisers in the Civil War, the second half of the seventeenth century saw the consolidation of their political power. Although the monarchy was restored in 1660, Parliament now held the upper hand. The subordination of the Crown to Parliament was established through the (largely bloodless) 'Glorious Revolution'[45] and enshrined by the Bill of Rights in 1689 – the progressive bourgeois interest now held the political power to complement its economic ascendency. The process of pushing the workers from the land in the pursuit of ever larger farms through enclosure was now resumed, but this time using the machinery of the state in the form of Parliamentary acts. Whereas Tudor enclosure had been piecemeal and resisted by the state, the process of Parliamentary Enclosure was the systematic, state-sponsored clearance of the people from the land on behalf of capitalist landowners. Through this mechanism almost 9 million (of England's 11 million) acres of farmland were redistributed from small-scale, subsistence workers to capitalist landowners by 1850. Local markets were freed from the regulation of the boroughs through a series of Acts from 1663.[46] Progress in financial markets and the judicial system promoted investment in longer-term projects which saw improvements to infrastructure, which in turn increased the viability of production for distant markets. The extent of navigable rivers, turnpike roads, canals and railways increased massively during this period.[47] Capitalism in England was in full swing and had been delivered by technological development, leading to a shift in production relations which in turn enabled further developments. The economic foundations of the old order had crumbled in the face of technological progress and the rise of the bourgeoisie. But there was no great revolutionary moment where the traditional aristocracy were swept away by the upstart capitalists. Although there had been bloodshed in the civil wars it mainly resulted from the inability of sections of the old order to embrace the changing world. There was a social, cultural and emotional investment in the traditional way of doing things which they couldn't forego – at least, not without a fight. As for the emerging capitalists – they were mainly drawn from the lower ranks of the feudal ruling class. The crucial revolutionary transformation was in the ownership relations – in the development of new class locations, rather than in the personnel occupying certain positions in the economic structure; in the emergence of a profit-seeking bourgeoisie and a propertyless proletariat. As Piketty has noted, 'In many ways the social and political regime that prevailed in the United Kingdom in the eighteenth and much of the nineteenth century represented a gradual fusion of aristocratic and proprietarian logics.'[48] Far from the capitalist upstarts putting the old feudal barons to the sword, the brunt of the suffering was borne by the workers – evicted from the land, subjected to persecution, forced to seek wage labour in the emerging industrial economy and drafted into service to be killed and maimed in the civil wars on both sides, though neither side was fighting for their interests. In Marx's words: 'Thus were the agricultural people, first forcibly expropriated from the soil, driven from their homes, turned into vagabonds, and then whipped, branded, tortured by laws grotesquely terrible, into the discipline necessary for the wage system.'[49] He lists numerous Acts of the sixteenth and seventeenth centuries specifying punishments including whipping, branding (variously on the breast, back, shoulder or forehead, depending on the 'crime'), cutting off half an ear, abduction of the transgressor's children into slavery, use of irons and manacles, imprisonment, slavery and execution. The birth of capitalism, particularly the clearance of the peasants from the land, can be a brutal process.

2.2 The Spread of Capitalism— France and the US

Across the Channel in France, technological developments – some imported from Britain – enabled a degree of progress in both agricultural and industrial production in the seventeenth and eighteenth centuries, but real transformation was hindered by the persistence of the *Ancien Régime* – the absolutism which the Stuart kings had tried to create in Britain, but had never quite achieved.[50]

As in England an emerging bourgeoisie, stifled by restrictions and exclusions, came into conflict with the backward-looking monarchy and nobility. There was some progress, of course. In 1627 Louis XIII had declared that maritime commerce would no longer 'stain the honour of a gentleman'. In 1767 this concession was extended to banking and manufacturing, but the French economic structure was still dominated by the nobility and clergy who between them owned 45 per cent of all the land in France, as well as claims to a proportion of the produce of much of the remainder.[51] As tensions broke out into conflict in the French Revolution from 1789, feudalism and the monarchy were abolished, Louis XVI was executed and the clergy and nobility had large portions of their land confiscated. We'll look at the process of confiscation and wider land reforms in Chapter 6 – for now it's important to note that, as in England, the bourgeoisie were asserting their dominance in French national life, and that the central processes were driven by technological advances and consisted of changes to the ways in which ownership was understood and distributed among the population. Although the regicide and *the terror* receive far more attention than the details of the conversions of feudal obligations into capitalist financial transactions, the latter were essential features of the revolutionary transformation, whereas the former were circumstantial – the revolution would still have been a revolution without them. Again as in England, regicide was not the final nail in the coffin of the French monarchy, the early republican years were plagued by personal rule and the transition from feudalism to capitalism included many twists and turns. During the process, bourgeois institutional change was exported far beyond the borders of France. With a population more than three times that of the UK, France was the dominant force in Europe and its transition to capitalism was felt across the continent, giving strength to emerging bourgeois interests in numerous countries. The wave of revolutions in 1848 and the establishment of bourgeois nation-states in the second half of the nineteenth century saw the spread of capitalism across Western Europe. By the beginning of the twentieth century the rise of the bourgeoisie had been consolidated and codified in constitutions across most of the continent. Often these arrangements included a compensatory nod to the representatives of the old order, accommodating their craving for status with ostentatious lifestyles, but with greatly reduced and often largely benign or merely ceremonial powers.

In the US there was no feudal yoke to overcome. The constitution was the product of Enlightenment ideals from the outset, with all the liberties – and contradictions – that entails.

The authors of the constitution didn't go so far as to outlaw slavery, and the agricultural economy of the *Land of the Free* was saddled with this hindrance to progress until abolition in 1865 following the Civil War. Although the slave economy was a major contributor to US exports and created a swathe of wealthy plantation owners across the Southern states, it was a suboptimal supplier of agricultural output to the world economy.[52] By definition, slave owners in the nineteenth century were not men of a progressive mindset, and they hindered the adoption of the flexible approach to labour and commodity production upon which the capitalist market thrives. Following the closure of the slave trade in 1807 there was virtually no attempt to attract free labour. The most prosperous slave states saw net outmigration throughout the period, even during cotton booms when demand for labour was high.[53] Infrastructure was neglected, inhibiting development, and plantations tended to aim for self-sufficiency in foodstuffs, which limited their capacity to produce for the market.[54] As the price of slaves rose after 1807 calls to re-open the slave trade – in order to meet the demands of the labour market – were resisted by slave owners, not out of any moral concern or any progressive desire to employ wage labour, but in order to protect the market value of their human 'assets'.[55] Wedded to the system that had created its wealth, staunchly opposed to progressive ideas and largely disinterested in modernisation, the slave-owning interest was incapable of adapting to the march of technological progress. As in England 200 years earlier, it was a civil war which finally saw the social and political hangovers of the past defeated by the economic demands of the future.[56]

Before we leave behind our survey of the historical transition from feudalism to capitalism there's one further example of this process we should look at. It's a case in point of the way in which the political ambitions of would-be authors of historical change can be derailed by long-term economic processes. It is the process by which feudalism in nineteenth-century Russia was transformed into the capitalism we see there today. I've dealt with this transition at length in *Unlearning Marx* and so here I'll provide only a brief summary.

2.3 The Russian Road to Capitalism

We've noted that the historical materialist concept of revolution does not equate to the sudden, violent political uprisings often called revolutions, but to the longer-term processes underlying those upheavals. This in turn helps us to avoid the idea that history consists of long periods of stability, punctuated by sudden revolutions which turn the world upside-down before receding into the background as a new epoch quickly settles in. Rather, the transition from one epoch to another is almost constantly at work. We've also noted that the progress through these epochal stages is constrained by the level of technological development at any given time – economic structures *correspond* to levels of development, as certain material conditions are required before each structure can take hold. For Marx, for example, there are certain technological prerequisites for the transition to socialism – including the condition that socialism would only be even a potential option in the most advanced capitalist societies. This is because it is capitalism which creates the 'ruthless productive powers of social labour, which alone can form the material basis for a free human society'.[57] Without capitalism having run its course – having fulfilled what he calls its 'historical task and justification'[58] – attempts to establish socialism would be doomed to failure. In Marx's words, full capitalist development is an 'absolutely necessary practical premise, because without it privation, *want* is merely made general, and with *want* the struggle for necessities would begin again, and all the old filthy business would necessarily be restored'.[59] Marx is here warning that if you try to distribute resources fairly, when the total amount of resources is insufficient, you merely distribute shortfall to everyone, so that no one has enough ('want is merely made general' i.e. not-having-enough is extended to the whole population), the struggle for necessities ensues and we end up back with 'all the old filthy business'. Russian revolutionaries had written to Marx in 1881 to ask if the Russian peasant commune might allow them to bypass the capitalist stage and leap straight into socialism. His answer was less than encouraging, though he did offer a potential way out in his Preface to the 1882 Russian edition of the *Communist Manifesto*. Here he suggested that a socialist revolution in Russia might succeed, but only if it acted as a catalyst for other socialist revolutions in the advanced capitalist nations.[60] Given the backward nature of Russia in 1917 and the failure of international revolutions to materialise, the Soviet failure is clearly explained (from this perspective) as a case of premature revolution, predictably failing to establish socialism, and ending in the restoration of 'all the old filthy business'.

But we can go further than that. Russia in 1917 was not only too backwards for socialism – it was insufficiently advanced even for capitalist production to take hold. Feudalism, as a formal system of serfdom, had survived longer in Tsarist Russia than in most of the rest of Europe. The legal emancipation of Russian serfs took place through a series of measures in the 1860s, but the terms of the emancipation kept the peasantry bound to the land and the landlords through a complex web of obligatory dues and duties. By 1917 capitalist production relations had penetrated the lives of no more than 10 per cent of Russian workers and peasants. The vast majority of immediate producers fell outside of our conception of proletarian status, either by virtue of their possession of relevantly significant means of production or because of their insufficient control over their own labour power. The 'expropriation of the great mass of the people from the soil, from the means of subsistence'[61] had not yet taken place. The means of production had not yet been 'transformed from the pygmy property of the many into the huge property of the few'.[62]

The absence of these fundamental preconditions of capitalist development restricted the progress of the capitalist mode of production. In terms of technological development, Russia had a long way to go before urbanisation or industrialisation could take place on any significant scale. In 1905 nearly three-quarters of Russian workers gave their main occupation as agriculture, fishing, hunting or lumbering.[63] At around 700 kg/ha, arable productivity in Russia in 1913 was lower than that attained in England by 1600.[64] Industry stumbled along, chiefly sponsored by the state or foreign capital – the absence of a proletariat in Tsarist Russia was matched by the weakness of the bourgeoisie. Russia was not ready for capitalism.

Amid the turmoil of the First World War Tsarism unexpectedly (and somewhat accidentally[65]) came to an end in February 1917. The Provisional Government proved inadequate and the Bolshevik faction of the RSDLP had seized political power by October. The declared aim of the Bolsheviks to establish socialism has led commentators from across the political spectrum to view the regime in those terms. But historians ought to be concerned with what people actually did, not what they said they were going to do, or what they claimed to be doing or even what they thought they were doing. The best efforts of Soviet propaganda can't hide the fact that the USSR never achieved a socialist economic structure.

In historical materialist terms, what they did achieve was to put in place all the prerequisites for capitalist development which had been absent in 1917. Permanently hamstrung by circumstances, the Soviet regime reacted to one crisis after another with policies focused on the urgent goal of survival. Having extricated the country from the First World War, it was then almost immediately attacked on all sides in a series of civil wars in which the counter-revolutionaries enjoyed support from Western governments. Emerging somehow victorious from this period of 'War Communism' by the beginning of

1921, the Bolsheviks now had the opportunity to embark on a peacetime programme of reform. The implementation of socialist policies, though, would have to wait. The chaos of war, revolution and more war had exacerbated the already poor productive output of the economy and the Bolsheviks were in no position to start directing the distribution of already insufficient resources. The regime had little option but to accept concessions to the market under a set of measures known as the New Economic Policy (NEP). A private sector was encouraged in industry and retail and markets in land and labour developed freely. The Soviets were stabilising the regime and consolidating their position, but modernisation was slow and the prospect of socialism or of revolutions in the West was receding all the time. Neither War Communism nor the NEP had moved the Soviet economy any closer to socialism.

Following Lenin's death (in 1924) and Stalin's rise to power, the NEP was abandoned by the end of 1929 in favour of a series of Five Year Plans under which impossibly ambitious targets were accompanied by brutal methods of requisitioning and forced collectivisation. While the aims of the Five Year Plans and collectivisation through state planning may have had acceptably socialist credentials, the end result – the expropriation of the peasantry and the concentration of their scattered plots into large-scale farms – is right out of Marx's list of prerequisites for the development of capitalism – disconnecting the peasants from the land, and consolidating their property into modern large-scale farms. Furthermore, the harsh methods of their implementation look very much like the grim realities of the equivalent process in Western Europe a few centuries earlier, which enabled the birth of capitalism and the acceleration of urbanisation and industrialisation.

By the time of Stalin's death in 1953 the economic prerequisites for the development of capitalism were all in place. Feudal bonds had been dissolved formally in the nineteenth century and in practice by the Bolsheviks under the NEP. The peasants had been forcibly expropriated from the land – their conception of rightful ownership had been broken by collectivisation, and would soon be a distant memory. The land had been transformed from the scattered and divided property of the peasantry into huge collective farms (*kolkhoz*) and state farms (*sovkhoz*), making the land ripe for conversion to capital a few generations later, as well as enabling some degree of mechanisation of agriculture. The increased yields resulting from this mechanisation enabled large-scale industrialisation and urbanisation, providing the material pre-condition for capitalism. All that was required now was the transfer of assets from the state into private hands...

As we noted earlier, a central claim of historical materialism is that although a given economic structure may promote development at a certain stage, it eventually will become a hindrance to further growth. The Soviet system had proved itself able to promote development from an immediately post-feudal level to that required for the emergence of a fully capitalist economy. But by the post-Stalin era the USSR found itself up against the advanced capitalist economies of the West, with which it could not compete. Western economies were reaching a level of development which was impossible within the Soviet model. While the Soviets could – in the short term – compete in terms of state-sponsored projects such as space exploration, the technology of the emerging digital age was led by consumer demand, and the planners could not hope to compete with the invisible hand of the market. The failure to meet consumer demand created a channel of internal disquiet aimed at the Soviet regime, alongside demands for religious freedom and resurgent nationalism. (Remember that the Soviet Union inherited the territory of the Russian Empire – only half the population were Russian nationals and the population of the USSR was drawn from over 100 nationalities.[66]) Internal tensions exacerbated the external pressures of the Cold War, which even in its later stages was a major drain on Soviet resources. As the regime wavered and debated over whether to adopt reforms along Swedish or Hungarian lines, prominent members of the establishment were positioning themselves to take advantage of the inevitable shift to private ownership. When privatisation came, these well-placed members of the Soviet machine – the *Nomenklatura* – took full advantage, subverting the various schemes aimed at distributing wealth and resources among the citizenry and creating a de facto class of capitalist oligarchs. Amid this process the Soviet Union was dissolved and political power passed to an ostensibly democratic system of government which few imagine serves the needs of anyone who doesn't own at least a coalfield or two.

So we can see that the course of Russian history has followed the path expected by historical materialist theory, despite some confusion caused by the 75-year interregnum under a regime claiming to be socialist, and under Stalin's policy of Socialism in One Country claiming to have subverted Marx's predictions and leapt over capitalism into socialism. From a feudal economic structure before the emancipation of the serfs in the 1860s to a capitalist economic structure by the end of the twentieth-century, Russia passed through the same processes we've identified as central to England's transformation a few centuries earlier, albeit under a very different guise.

2.4 Revolution and Reform

A question which has faced the left for generations is that of 'Revolution or Reform?' Despite the volume and intensity of debates around this question, it's almost always framed incorrectly. It's usually taken in the context of *means* – should we be on the streets with Molotov cocktails or taking a parliamentary route, lobbying our MPs and signing petitions? But 'revolution or reform' is really a question of *ends* – can capitalism be reformed until justice is achieved or must it be replaced with a different economic structure? It's emphatically **not** the case that violent regime change necessarily constitutes revolution, any more than it's the case that gradual change is limited to reformist ambitions. As we've seen, a revolution, such as the one which ushered in capitalism, can be a long, incremental process. By the same token it's entirely possible for a sudden, violent seizure of political power to merely impose new personnel into existing roles – leaving the economic structure intact and having no revolutionary impact at all. Advocating the removal of capitalism doesn't require one to hold unrealistic ideas about the likelihood of an insurrection – even less so about its desirability or chances of success. It's not a contradiction to take a gradualist approach to realising revolutionary ambitions. Such an approach is not only more philosophically, historically and strategically viable but also far more realistic than ideas about an armed uprising. Defending such a revolution would be impossible, but even seizing power in the first place is a pipe dream. In the lyrics of *Five to One* Jim Morrison tells us 'they've got the guns, but we've got the numbers'. In truth, we don't even have the numbers. We didn't then (in 1968) and we don't now. And 'they' don't just have guns. They have drones. And helicopter gunships and body armour and tanks. They have a trained fighting force and bunkers and space age communication facilities. All those survivalists up in the mountains of Idaho with an arsenal of Uzis and a million rounds each wouldn't last 5 minutes against the US armed forces – what odds do you give the Tooting Popular Front? In Russia in 1917 the army – largely composed of conscripts, and demoralised from 3 years on the wrong end of the *Great War* hostilities, led by donkeys and ill-equipped by an anachronistic regime – became a hotbed of revolutionary ferment. The situation in the UK and US today couldn't be more different. As well as being theoretically misplaced and strategically counter-productive the idea of an armed uprising leading to a seizure of power and a period of consolidation is pure fantasy.

Marxist academic David Harvey has recently (August 2020) argued that capitalism is 'too big to fail'.[67] By this he means that a sudden overthrow of capitalism would cause such disruptions to supply chains across the world that many of the most vulnerable people – the very people such an overthrow purports to help – would suffer catastrophic destruction to their lives. While this has been received by many on the anti-capitalist left as some sort of surrender or capitulation, it is no such thing. It's merely the recognition of reality. Although I'd disagree with some of the detail of Harvey's analysis (and the phrase 'too big to fail' doesn't quite describe my position) it's undeniable that a sudden upheaval would cause considerable suffering to many of the least well off in the world. Global capitalism is an incredibly complex system and most of the forces for good in the world are inextricably intertwined with capitalist institutions. Supply chains for food and medicine, international aid, vaccination programmes, education and research facilities, support for victims of crime and abuse – there's an almost endless list of worthwhile and essential services which need to remain uninterrupted in the progression away from a capitalist economic structure and that can only happen through the kind of incremental process which characterised the transition from feudalism into capitalism. That is one of the reasons why the final section of this volume (chapters 7-10) presents measures aimed at progressing us away from capitalism, rather than at suddenly overthrowing it.

The criticism of Harvey's position comes in two flavours – on the one hand that his analysis is incorrect and on the other that his position is a deviation from Marx. Critics are sometimes confused about which criticism they're making, and some apparently think that *being incorrect* and *deviating from Marx* are just two descriptions of the same thing. While the value of the analysis is the really important thing, and whether or not it's a deviation from Marx is of merely historical interest, it's worth quickly noting that Marx's attachment to the concept of a forceful overthrow of capitalism has been regularly overstated from commentators across the political spectrum.[68] To *any* observer in the middle of the nineteenth century, it would have seemed obvious that the most likely way – perhaps the only way – in which the mass of people could achieve a system in which their stake in society was recognised would be through the use of force. The significant examples of seizures of political power available to people of that time were those bloodthirsty episodes carried out by bourgeois interests in England in the seventeenth century and France in the eighteenth. The civil wars of the 1640s cost a higher proportion of English lives than both the first and second world wars combined. The 'revolutionary' period in France was not short on bloodshed while the export of bourgeois interests and the assault on embedded European powers continued for decades and left millions of casualties. The seizures of political power that accompanied the capitalist revolutions were murderous affairs – why would anyone expect future revolutions to be any different?

And yet, later in life, Marx noted the expansion of political participation and spoke favourably of the potential of democracy to provide a vehicle for structural change. Even by the end of his life there wasn't a single example of a country with a democratic electoral system. (Universal adult suffrage was first adopted in New Zealand in 1893, 10 years after Marx died.) As early as 1871, though, he noted that, 'In England, for instance, the way to show political power lies open to the working class. Insurrection would be madness where peaceful agitation would more swiftly and surely do the work.'[69] The following year he argued in a speech in Amsterdam that 'there are countries – such as America, England, and if I were more familiar with your institutions, I would perhaps also add Holland – where the workers can attain their goal by peaceful means'.[70]

In this chapter I have referred often to the progressive and traditionalist tendencies among the outgoing feudal class and described how the progressive wing introduced new technology, established bourgeois production relations and finally overhauled the political system to further accommodate their ascendency. I've avoided using familiar political labels to describe these groups and processes, because to do so is misleading. Political culture is something which is imperfectly overlaid on top of the economic power relations in a society. In Chapter 4 we'll look at how various political positions map onto these economic relations and the evolution of the current political landscape, from the Whigs, Tories and radicals to neo-cons, democratic socialists and beyond. The most important thing to note for now is that the correspondence between political ideology and a role in a revolutionary process is not straightforward. During the crisis that led to the Glorious Revolution, those favouring a strong parliament and a constitutional monarchy with limited powers became known as *Whigs*, and their opponents, supporting the Stuart kings and their tendency to absolutism became known as the *Tories*. But although the Whigs were predominantly promoting the bourgeois agenda of merchants and industrialists, they drew considerable support from the old aristocratic families of England. On the other hand, their opposition, the Tories (still a parliamentary grouping, rather than a party in the modern sense) included landowners of progressive, as well as traditional, outlook. They may have been forward-looking when it came to the operation of their farms, but socially and culturally they were still embedded in the fabric of rural society – big fish in small ponds who resisted radical *social* and *cultural* change, unless it was clearly to their benefit.

The point here is that people are often unaware of the great processes of historical change going on around them and in which their lives are caught up. The motives they profess can be quite genuine even though, with the benefit of distance and hindsight, we can see that their actions – collectively – created conditions beyond their intentions – sometimes far removed from those intentions. The transformation from feudalism to capitalism – the bourgeois revolution – was not anyone's plan, but consisted of an aggregation of incalculable individual actions and decisions, each made with the intention of meeting relatively short-term and often quite personal aims.

Those familiar with historical materialism may be wondering where this type of explanation of historical change accommodates the familiar concepts of class consciousness and class action. Isn't a Marxist revolution supposed to involve the radicalised proletariat rising up and forcibly overthrowing the bourgeois overlords? Well, no, not necessarily. In Marx's more political and journalistic works he sometimes called for such an insurrection, but in his more considered, theoretical writing it's clear that he views the process of transformation as one of changing economic relationships driven by technological developments. The political upheavals we've noted – the English Civil War, the French Revolution and so on – are flashpoints in the transformation but do not constitute the transformation itself. For Marx, explanations which give political upheavals explanatory primacy over economic changes are back to front – the political tail is wagging the economic dog.

Viewed from this perspective, a 'revolutionary course of action' doesn't always involve storming the Bastille or detaching a monarch's head from his body. In historical materialist explanations, the 'era of social revolution' is essentially characterised by the displacement of one dominant production relation by another. It is possible that this revolution could consist entirely of processes of 'adaptive metamorphosis' or revolution from above. Indeed, Marx's description of the emergence of capitalism in England includes elements of both of these processes. He describes how 'the great feudal lords created an incomparably larger proletariat by the driving of the peasantry from the land'[71] and how they then 'vindicated for themselves the rights of modern private property in estates to which they had only a feudal title'.[72] In this way the feudal landowners were able to deliver 'what the capitalist system demanded...a degraded and almost servile condition of the mass of the people, the transformation of them into mercenaries and of their means of labour into capital'.[73] Thus the bourgeois revolution is carried through, in part at least, by the actions of members of the feudal class in transforming themselves into members of the bourgeoisie (placing their operations on a capitalist basis), and, in the process, transforming the peasantry into a proletariat; free from feudal obligations and 'free from, unencumbered by, any means of production of their own'.[74] The bourgeois revolution in England involved a wide variety of forms of 'revolutionary action', and a broad range of 'revolutionaries', including feudal landowners. In Chapter 3 we'll look more at the way in which people's ownership or non-ownership of productive resources can influence the range of actions open to them and their likely motivations for supporting various approaches to change.

2.5 Economic Determinism

A criticism often levelled at historical materialism is that it is a form of economic determinism. The suggestion is that it crudely reduces all human interactions to their economic aspect. Thomas Piketty, for example, takes issue with Marxist approaches in which the economic base determines the superstructure in an almost mechanical way insisting 'that the realm of ideas, the political-ideological sphere, is truly autonomous'.[75] Elsewhere, however, he concedes that ideologies emerge in order to defend and legitimise the existing economic structure. Referring to Medieval Europe he argues that 'the primary goal was to justify existing social hierarchies so that the *laboratores* would accept their lot and understand that, as good Christians here below, they were obliged to respect the ternary order and therefore the authority of the clergy and nobility'.[76] This latter statement seems to acknowledge that such ideologies are not wholly autonomous but arise and persist because of the functional advantage they provide for existing economic and political interests. Of course, Piketty is right to be wary of reductionist arguments which ignore the 'complexity and flux of human affairs'[77] but it's possible to maintain an approach which recognises the fundamental importance of technological developments and economic relations without forcing every detail into an explanatory straightjacket.

The account of Russian history given above provides a good illustration of the way in which economic factors are held to be fundamental drivers of change, but are not considered to be all-encompassing in determining the exact course of history. It's worth reviewing our earlier summary of the process of historical change:

- historical change is driven by technological development
- various economic structures arise and persist because they promote development
- as technology develops, an economic structure that had previously promoted development may now hinder further development
- in such a case, the economic structure will (eventually) give way, and be replaced with a new economic structure which promotes further development. If economic structures sometimes impede further development, and if rationality dictates that development cannot be subverted indefinitely – then economic structures must 'rise and fall...as they enable or impede that growth'.[78]

The only really *deterministic* proposal here is that development cannot be subverted indefinitely, a claim which arises simply from the assertion of the Development Thesis that humans are sufficiently ingenious as to be able to improve their lives, and sufficiently rational as to not reject the opportunity to do so (temporary bouts of irrationally rejecting progress for religious or other cultural reasons notwithstanding).

Obviously historical materialism doesn't predict or dictate the actual events by which this process will manifest itself. In the case of Russia, had Nicholas II been less incompetent or his brother Archduke Michael been less reluctant, perhaps Tsarism may have persisted and overseen a transition to capitalism (though it's unlikely that it would have survived the transition unless the Romanovs could have found it in themselves to embrace a constitutionally limited role). Had the Provisional Government enjoyed better leadership, then perhaps after the Great War Russia could have overcome its past and its backwardness and embarked on a gradual path to capitalism. Had Lenin lived longer, or Stalin been thwarted in his ambitions, perhaps a continuation of NEP into more conciliatory Five Year Plans may have prepared the ground for capitalism through a less traumatic twentieth-century. (Though this may have weakened the Soviet position against Hitler's invasion in the Second World War.) Perhaps, without Soviet direction, Russia would have failed to develop the preconditions for capitalism and become imperially or commercially subjugated to the advanced Western powers. Or perhaps a typical proto-bourgeois middle class may have developed and set in motion a more traditional bourgeois revolution. The development of capitalism was not inevitable, but once it had emerged elsewhere and proved itself far more efficient than any available options (given the level of technological development at the time), one way or another, capitalism was coming to Russia. As it happens, Russia's bourgeois revolution was carried out largely by the Soviet regime's pursuit of survival and modernisation.

In the case of the US, while the Civil War was clearly a significant moment in the process of abolishing slavery in North America, there should be no suggestion that had war been avoided, or if the Confederacy had won, that slavery would still be with us now. At some point, the inefficiency of slave-based agriculture would have been usurped by more efficient capitalist agricultural production – whether by war or simply by economic reality. Similarly, to argue that the English Civil War was a decisive moment in the course of English history would be to suggest that (for example) had Prince Rupert not lost his discipline at the Battle of Edgehill, on a Sunday afternoon in 1642, and the Royalists had prevailed, then the march of industrialisation, capitalism and democracy might have been stopped in its tracks. Despite the clear absurdity of this position, it is directly entailed by the 'great men', battles and dates approach to history taught in schools and perpetuated by the majority of popular historical broadcasting. This approach doesn't deny Piketty's assertion of 'the complexity and multiplicity of the political and ideological pathways we actually observe in different countries and regions' but it does suggest that the economic base underlying those pathways will be able to make the most of current technology – or will soon give way to a structure that does.[79]

In this chapter, then, we've taken the theoretical framework we covered in Chapter 1 and looked at how it applies to real-world examples of historical change. Of course, there are many different ways to look at the same events, and they're not necessarily mutually exclusive, but given the general levels of confusion about what's going on in the world, and where we might be going, it seems to me a valuable project to take a framework that provides an insightful view of past developments, and see whether it could apply to future developments too. In Chapter 3 we'll review some aspects of our current situation and ask whether they suggest that we're approaching a period of transition away from capitalism. We'll also discuss whether people's class location – that is their ownership or non-ownership of productive resources – might influence their motivation for supporting various avenues of change.

3

Capitalism Undone

The history of the twentieth century encourages the thought that the easiest way to generate productivity in a modern society is by nourishing the motives of greed and fear. But we should never forget that greed and fear are repugnant motives.
G.A. Cohen, 2009[80]

Capitalism, then, can be viewed as an economic structure capable of developing productive capacity to previously unimagined levels, and defined by its dominant production relations in which most people own no productive resources of their own, and as such must sell their labour power on the open market. Such workers are free from the obligations of pre-capitalist workers, as well as being free from ('unencumbered by'[81]) any ownership of the means of production.

3.1 Does Capitalism Still Work?

Despite its obvious shortcomings, huge swathes of the world's population have benefitted from the productive advances of the capitalist era in terms of improved nutrition, health, housing, infrastructure and services. While the distribution of such benefits has been vastly uneven, and the management of the process often brutal, improvements have been felt across a broad mass of people at various levels of wealth and income. Such benefits have not been the aim of capitalism or even of capitalists, but the drive to continually accumulate more capital and thus to increase productive capacity has obviously had beneficial side-effects in terms of the volume and variety of products available to people. (Capitalists don't set out to satisfy your needs, but to make money – but the fastest way to make money is to satisfy your needs better than anyone else, providing, of course, that you have money to exchange in return for such a service. If you have no money, capitalists aren't interested in your needs or wants.) As a result, opposition to capitalism has been blunted in many circumstances as people are reluctant to bite the (invisible) hand that feeds them. And yet there's a limit to the correlation whereby chasing profit happens to produce outcomes favourable to enough people to maintain sufficient support for a profit-driven system. A point is reached at which the self-interest of resource owners stops coinciding with the development of greater productive capacity and the output of the capitalist system ceases to meet any interpretation of the wants and needs of the population. Both of these processes are clearly evident within today's advanced economies, and between these economies and those of the developing world.

The growing financial sector in the US now accounts for around a third of GDP[82] and this situation is mirrored across the globe to some degree. For many capitalists the fastest and easiest way to accumulate capital is not to provide goods or services that people need, but to speculate in the financial markets, which is far from beneficial to our economic performance. Commenting on financialisation of the US economy, Michael Hudson notes, 'The financial sector's aim is not to minimize the costs of roads, electric power, transportation, water or education, but to maximize what can be charged as monopoly rent.'[83] Joseph Stiglitz goes further: 'The financial sector is emblematic of what has gone wrong in our economy – a major contributor to the growth of inequality, the major source of instability in our economy, and an important cause of the economy's poor performance over the last three decades.'[84] In the UK, according to Ann Pettifor, 'We are living through a disastrous era in which the financial sector has expanded vastly – an era in which most financiers have virtually no direct relationship to the real economy's production of goods and services.'[85] This is not a phenomenon unique to the Anglosphere – as James Galbraith has demonstrated, there's a clear link between increasing financialisation of the world's economies and the growth of global inequality.[86] The financial sector produces little, excludes many, destabilises the economy and increases inequality. Its growth is a hindrance to progress, not a facilitator.

Of course, under global capitalism, financial markets provide some of the investment required for companies providing goods and services, but again here we see a move away from the model whereby profit is generated by meeting people's needs. The affiliate marketing industry, for example – one of the 'success stories' of the internet age – actually hinders the process whereby producers and consumers encounter each other in the marketplace.[87] Whereas traditional advertising – as well as peddling lies about diesel emissions and tobacco – might be seen as performing the useful role of directing a consumer with a need, to a company with a product to satisfy that need, affiliate marketing does no such thing. Much affiliate marketing works by scraping a slim profit from transactions by hijacking the consumer's online search and inserting extra steps between the customer and the commodity. This huge industry produces nothing of worth and actually hinders the process of discovery. Thousands of people, millions of workhours, office buildings, heating, lighting, pollution, congestion – and at the end of the day not a single additional product is created or useful service delivered. Money moves from account *a* to account *b*, but no need or want is met – there are no more chairs or tables in the world, no more tricycles, trombones or trampolines. No more satisfied customers – affiliate marketing usually makes it *harder* to find what you want. This self-interested, money-making behaviour of rational economic actors makes zero impact on the level of development of the productive forces – nor is it of any material benefit to anyone. The 'pie' is not in any meaningful sense any bigger as a result of this activity. In the world of affiliate marketing, the invisible hand of the market delivers nothing but a minor redistribution of zeros and ones among computerised bank balances.

Even when actual physical products are created it's hard to argue that the output of much of the capitalist economy still coincides with any interpretation of the concept of progress. One of capitalism's strengths has always been its ability to rapidly adjust to circumstances – profit was made by satisfying demand. But today, in many industries we're *manufacturing* demand, not meeting it. We have disposable razors with seven blades, the top dozen brands of washing powder are all made by two manufacturers and the *Danny DeVito Celebrity Prayer Candle* is a thing. In December 2019 arch-capitalist UK newspaper *The Daily Telegraph* ran a piece asking if the world really needs 15 different Harry Potter Advent Calendars.[88] When even *Telegraph* journalists are questioning the outcome of leaving everything to the market it's time to wonder if things have gone too far. Yet still we have R & D departments coming up with ways to create razors with eight blades, advertising agencies trying to differentiate almost identical products through the promotion of endless brands, and marketing departments trying to predict whether an Angela Merkel novelty worship accessory would outsell Louis Theroux. At the same time we have collapsing infrastructure, chronic staff shortages in the NHS and over 100,000 vacancies in the UK social care sector. There is a striking mismatch between our needs and the allocation of our resources. Maybe the invisible hand of the market isn't so unerringly accurate after all?

The global situation is no better. While 9 million people die of hunger and related causes every year, we throw away 1.3 billion tonnes of food. According to the UN, 28 per cent of the world's agricultural area is used annually to produce food that is lost or wasted.[89] It's the twenty-first century. We can do better than this.

Supporters of capitalism argue that almost by definition there cannot be a more efficient system of meeting needs than the mechanisms of the free market. Even though the sole aim of the capitalist is to make money, not to satisfy needs – they can only make money by satisfying needs – and doing so more efficiently than anyone else. (Though we should remember that the only needs the market ever addresses are those backed by the ability to pay.) Capitalism automatically selects out, so the story goes, the inefficient producers. In this limited context, the concept of the efficiency of the market was possibly true in the 1870s. Even in the 1950s the pads and pens and filing cabinets of Soviet Gosplanners couldn't compete with market mechanisms in the West for predicting and meeting consumer demand. But we've noted the domination of the unproductive financial sector, the rise of parasitical sectors such as affiliate marketing, the absurdities on our supermarket shelves and the waste of nearly a quarter of our food while millions die of hunger every year. Given all of that, it's astounding that the idea of the market as the super-efficient arbiter of production and distribution retains any credibility at all in the twenty-first century. We live in a different world now and the market is falling short. The connection between what makes money for capitalists and what advances civilisation has come unstuck. Perhaps we should set out with the aim of catering for people's real needs, regardless of their ability to pay for their subsistence, rather than trying to cater for the ambitions of entrepreneurs to buy more yachts and hoping that the starving might be fed as a by-product of that process. Perhaps twenty-first century computing power might be able to help us with that – it seems to be pretty good at targeting Facebook users with deceptive political campaigns – maybe we should see if Cambridge Analytica could target hungry people with food? It might even be a possibility that – if we get our skates on – we can cut out all this waste while we still have a functioning planet!

I should be clear here – I'm not advocating Soviet-style central planning. I'm making the point that when capitalism is defended on the grounds that it has developed productive capacity and brought untold abundance to the world through the efficiency of the market (to the extent that it is true at all) that is a defence of its record in the past – there's no guarantee that it will continue to be so beneficial in the future and, indeed, all the signs are that capitalism has already outlived its usefulness. Claims that the less well-off members of capitalist societies receive sufficient benefits from economic growth to outweigh the iniquities of the growth-promoting system no longer stand up to scrutiny. While the 'pie' has continued to increase in size, the benefits have become ever more concentrated. In the US, for example, between 1989 and 2019 overall household wealth more than doubled (after adjusting for inflation and population growth), but while the richest 40 per cent gained considerably (with the richest 20 per cent making by-far the highest gains) the wealth of the poorest 40 per cent of households decreased and the middle 20 per cent remained almost static. Note that this is the actual *wealth*, not the *share* belonging to the poorest households.[90]

3.2 Capitalism and Rationality

It's all very well to argue that capitalism is producing 'irrational' outcomes – that humankind is no longer reaping sufficient aggregated rewards from the system to justify its continued dominance. But, in the absence of some global mechanism by which we can all agree to move on, how will widespread dissatisfaction turn into a move away from the current economic structure? Recall that the transition from feudalism into capitalism was no one's plan, but the sum of countless decisions made by many individuals, across generations. Technological developments created new possibilities and for individuals to grasp those possibilities was rational, given the location of the decision-makers in the network of ownership relations.

Is it the case, then, that current technological developments are increasing the number of people whose needs and wants are no longer being met by capitalism? (Adding to the very many whose needs and wants have never been met by capitalism.) And are there courses of action open to these people which could contribute to a shift away from the capitalist economic structure? At this point I'd like to look at two areas in which recent and imminent developments are creating just this situation. In both cases the processes are not new, but in each of them recent developments mean that their impact on society is unprecedented.

3.3 *Automation and Artificial Intelligence*

The first proposed mechanism is simply the drastically changing scale and scope of the impact of technology in the workplace. Since the Luddites[91] and the Swing Riots[92] in the early nineteenth century, workers have opposed automation. Technological advances have resulted in unemployment and destitution across a range of industries since the earliest days of the factory system, and – coupled with the export of manufacturing to the developing world – have sent recurring shockwaves through working-class communities in the West.

For those in the poorly-rewarded jobs traditionally usurped by progress, this is nothing new, and illustrates one of the absurdities of capitalist production – that those whose lives are blighted by drudgery and toil have learnt to fear the invention of any machine that might decrease the amount of drudgery and toil they are required to suffer. Technological advances which result in a reduction in the amount of work required to produce the same outcome should be welcomed by all, but we've been conditioned under capitalism to fear such progress. In the 1970s and 1980s many trade unionists opposed both environmentalism and nuclear disarmament because of the perceived threat to jobs. In 2006 Barack Obama argued that private health insurance must be retained in the US because otherwise 2 or 3 million jobs in health insurance would be lost, even though the tasks undertaken by those workers would not be necessary under a nationalised system. Essentially, as we noted in the introduction, he was proposing that a public system would be more efficient and require less paperwork, but couldn't be adopted because it would be more efficient and require less paperwork.[93] Today, social media posts do the rounds imploring people not to use self-service checkouts at supermarkets because they're putting cashiers out of work. While these responses are entirely understandable from the point of view of those facing unemployment, as a society it's time to recognise that less work to be done isn't a bad thing – it's the wages that people fear the loss of, not the drudgery and toil. We need to move into a situation where machines can do the work without causing humans to become destitute. It seems incredulous that this should even need to be said, but apparently it does. Many, if not most, low-income jobs are largely disagreeable. Of course, there are often elements of work that people enjoy – the social aspect, the feeling of accomplishment and of having contributed – but 45 years of 40 hours a week on the nightshift at a mattress factory for barely enough money to keep the wolves from the door isn't the extent of anyone's life's ambition – and if it is, then it really shouldn't be. Even in 1932 Bertrand Russell argued that, 'The fact is that moving matter about (while a certain amount of it is necessary for our existence) is emphatically not one of the ends of human life.' Russell notes that we have been misled by those who 'preach the dignity of labour, while taking care themselves to remain undignified in this respect'.[94]

The difference today is the range as well as the number of jobs being replaced by technological advances. Of course automation is still adversely affecting low-wage employment as it always has done, but now artificial intelligence (AI) is supplanting automation with medium- and high-tech jobs coming under threat:

> Workers with graduate or professional degrees will be almost four times as exposed to AI as workers with just a high school degree. Holders of bachelor's degrees will be the most likely to be made redundant – facing more exposure than any other group by education level, more than five times as exposed to AI than workers with just a high school degree.[95]

Vulnerability to the effects of AI increases through the range of wage-income levels, right up to the ninetieth percentile and the impact is likely to be felt not only by a broader range of skill-sets and income levels, but also across a more diverse group of industries. According to Michael Webb's extensive and innovative research (itself using AI to compare the scope of AI patents with tasks listed in job descriptions in the labour market) the only sectors in which the impact of AI will be negligible are those in which face-to-face contact is an asset, such as health care, social services and education.[96]

The importance of the fact that AI will affect higher-paid roles than was the case with automation is not that those roles are more valuable or that the people that occupy them are more worthy of our sympathy, it's largely that the impact will be much wider and as with all things, there is a tipping point to be reached before anything changes. It's also true that the impact of AI will be felt by people with more influence, more access to the media, more contacts among decision-makers. The main thing is that the number of people whose livelihoods are threatened by AI is far greater than any previous wave of occupational displacement. More people than ever before in the advanced capitalist nations will find that the system requires little from them and has little to offer them in return.

While earlier waves of technologically driven occupational displacement largely affected powerless or isolated groups such as weavers in the 1830s or print workers in the 1980s, the AI revolution will cause disruption across almost all groups who rely on wages for their income. The scale of the impact of these developments will make it necessary to adopt a new approach to coping with the effects of technology. The Luddites and the print workers did their best to resist change, but the response that is now required is to accept change, and to work out how to live with it. This can only be achieved on a society-wide scale, and doing so will require a fundamental rethinking of our relationship with work and therefore of our concept of the relationship between work and reward. These issues are discussed further in Chapter 7.

3.4 Rescuing the Proletariat

There's an element to all of this which has important consequences for the relevance of Marx's analysis of class, and its role in transformative change. The combination of automation and AI will hit workers in all sectors, of all ages, with all levels of qualification and at all income levels up to the ninetieth percentile. While this encompasses individuals as diverse as 50-year-old supermarket cashiers and 20-something data analysts, all of these people have something in common. They must all work for a living, and they must all do so because they lack sufficient ownership or control of resources to be able to live without working. They are proletarians, and the conditions of their existence which define them as proletarians are the same conditions of existence which – in the face of being forced out of the employment market – will make it more likely that they will support alternatives to the capitalist mantra *work or starve*. (Or in societies with a social safety net, 'Work or be really poor.')

For generations, the stratification of the proletariat – the steadily increasing affluence of a subset of paid employees, has been taken as proof that class consciousness was a dead duck. Commentators waxed lyrical about the upward social mobility of a proportion of the children of manual workers – largely to fill new white-collar positions created by the switch to a service and information economy as manufacturing and agriculture have been increasingly mechanised and exported to the developing world. In the 1960s sociologists debated whether workers were becoming 'middle class' now that they could afford consumer durables such as washing machines. From this point of view 'affluence was held to be associated with a process of embourgeoisement, of which increased Conservative voting among manual workers was an important part'.[97] In turn this idea was rebutted with the argument that people making their lives easier by buying consumer durables was not necessarily a symptom of changing class identities or loyalties, but was just a symptom of people wanting to make their lives easier by buying consumer durables – as David Lockwood put it, 'A washing machine is a washing machine is a washing machine.'[98] All of this makes some sense if you view class as something related to income, or aspiration, or consumer goods, or where people shop or what car they drive. But that approach completely fails to accommodate the shared experience of proletarians in a range of occupations in the face of technologically driven displacement from the employment market. Here a structural view of class is what we need to understand how these technological developments will impact proletarians across all income, education and skill ranges. As the post-war economy evolved people became less likely to work in a traditional industry or in a large workforce, to do manual work, to belong to a trade union or to live in a council house. But these changes have not affected all 'working-class' people to the same degree, hence the social stratification of the traditional working class and the idea that class solidarity and class consciousness are things of the past. But, as we noted in Chapter 1, a historical materialist analysis doesn't deal in concepts such as 'the working class', but prefers a more structural category – the proletariat. Defined not by income levels, or skill levels or by the colour of their collars, the proletariat are those who – because of their non-ownership of any means of production – must sell their labour power in order to escape destitution. This group includes many who live relatively comfortable lives, but none who could survive long-term unemployment in anything but desperate circumstances. For proletarians social stratification is intimately bound up with employment stratification, and widespread unemployment removes many of the trappings of that stratification. After a few months on the dole, the material circumstances of the unemployed accountant and the unemployed welder begin to converge, as does the range of behaviours that make sense, given those circumstances.

In our earlier review of the revolution which ushered in the capitalist era I argued that we need to accept that there's a much broader range of behaviours that can be considered to be 'revolutionary acts' than is often thought. A revolutionary act in this sense includes those we noted in the bourgeois revolutions – evicting tenants from copyhold tenures, enclosing common land and so on (with no Molotov cocktails in sight). In a similar vein, we also need to rethink the range of ways in which individual motivations could relate to a person's class location. The bourgeois revolution was not carried out by people conscious of their class situation and acting collectively to promote their class interests. However, the individual actions which contributed to the process of transition were often motivated by material circumstances – by the nature and extent of individuals' ownership of means of production. Similarly, those who may become under-employed or unemployed (or in some cases unemployable) by automation and AI share the common situation of being financially dependent on wages. With no ownership of means of production to fall back on, many people – even those on relatively comfortable salaries – depend on their ability to earn in order to keep paying the bills. Stratification of income and of lifestyles might lead to social, cultural and political differences while unemployment is low and concentrated on the most vulnerable, but the structural condition of proletarian status will encourage a wide range of workers to support ideas such as Universal Basic Income or a jobs guarantee scheme as a greater range of occupations become obsolete in the face of technological progress. (Both Universal Basic Income (UBI) and the concept of a job-guarantee scheme are discussed in chapters 8 and 9.)

Of course, real life is always more complex than ideal-typical concepts and numerous shades exist in reality where our model sees only definitive lines. One group, which we may call the *technocracy*, can be said to have effectively left proletarian status behind, although they remain wage-earning employees. There is some overlap between this class and the group known as the Professional Managerial Class, but they are not identical categories. In *Unlearning Marx* I provide an extensive analysis of the class location of this well-paid, wage-earning technocracy and discuss at some length the distinctions between this group and both the proletariat and the petty-bourgeoisie.[99] (As the name suggests, the petty-bourgeoisie are the small business owners who own enough capital to be self-employed but not enough to free themselves from the obligation to work.)[100] It's important to note that the technocracy are not excluded from the proletariat because they earn too much money, or because they enjoy a large degree of autonomy in their work. It is the effective (though incomplete) control they exercise over productive assets by virtue of their technical knowledge that separates them from the proletariat. They make largely autonomous decisions about how and where productive assets will be deployed, and the expert knowledge which gives them the ability to do so puts them in a different relationship to both the means of production and to the bourgeoisie than that of the proletarian. At the same time, they do not enjoy the full range of ownership rights over the assets they control – they cannot sell or bequeath them for example. This limitation sets them apart from the petty-bourgeoisie. In relatively stable times the interests of the technocrats may not coincide with those of proletarians, particularly those at the lower end of income and autonomy scales, but if predictions of the impact of AI on many technical roles are correct, we might find that the two groups have more in common than they had thought. After all, the factors which differentiate the technocrats from the proletarians are conditional upon their employment. An unemployed architect or geologist has as much interest in UBI or a jobs guarantee as an unemployed miner or mechanic. While these technological advances might bring to light similarities in the interests of the technocracy with the proletariat, they are also likely to emphasise the differences between the interests of the technocracy and the petty-bourgeoisie. A jobs guarantee, for example, represents an increase in government spending into the economy. For technocrats, this might provide a host of new employment opportunities, whereas such a policy is more likely to be opposed by the petty-bourgeoisie, for whom it could provide competition in the employment market, and an increase in costs.

As progress begins to detach the whole range of salaried employees from the workplace, more and more of us might come to view this process as an opportunity, not a catastrophe. Less work! That's what capitalism was supposed to be for! To drive productive capacity and technological development to the point where it is 'no longer true that most of life and time and energy must be spent joylessly producing means to imperative ends'.[101] But this freedom which capitalism enables cannot be *delivered by* capitalism. Taking Adam Smith's famous example of a pin factory, Bertrand Russell illustrates the point. If a machine is invented which enables the manufacture of the same number of pins with half of the labour input, capitalism allows only one way to proceed: half the labour force are turfed out into destitution, while the other half continue to work their fingers to the bone.[102] A sane society, Russell argues, would surely respond to this situation by allowing all of the workers to work half days. The same number of pins will be produced, they will sell for the same amount of money, the capitalist will still take his profit, the workers will still be paid, and the machine which was invented to halve the work will have done just that – to much rejoicing from the workers. The problem with this assessment is that Russell has completely failed to understand the nature of technological progress under capitalism – the very feature which makes it so much more productive and inventive than any other system.[103] Under capitalism the machine wasn't invented to halve the work. It was invented to halve the costs. That is how capitalism works – and, in Marx's terms, it's *why* capitalism works. From this perspective, the point of capitalism is the unprecedented development of technology, the rapid expansion of productive capacity, the route out of scarcity – the delivery of abundance.

It will help to look at the way an entrepreneur might critique Russell's argument. Firstly, he talks about the pin factory as if the machine that halved the work must also halve the cost, but that's not true. The machine required some capital investment, which had to come from somewhere. While the ongoing savings may be 50 per cent, there's some initial investment to return. That's okay – Russell might reply – we can adjust our figures slightly to factor that in. (Perhaps the workers could work 55 per cent of their previous hours over the lifetime of the machine to cover the costs.) But that's not really the main objection to Russell's position. The more important point is that the invention of the machine required time and effort to be spent by someone with the possibility of no reward. What if it turned out that a pin-making machine can't be made? Or if it breaks so often as to be no cheaper than labour? Under capitalism, the inventor of the machine – and his entrepreneurial backers – need to know that the rewards for inventing such a contraption make that risk of failure worthwhile. The rewards must be extraordinary otherwise no one will risk the investment. Capitalism provides for just such extraordinary rewards, which is exactly why it cannot be supplanted until it has driven us to the point of abundance – and why, having reached that point, it becomes obsolete. We now have enough productive capacity to keep us supplied in pins – and in suitcases, and bicycles and banjos. We have passed the point where our problem is that we have an insufficient volume of things. Our problems now revolve around the organisation of employment and production and the distribution of who produces and of what's produced. Our problems now are that we have too many people for the work available, and that we have work that we all want to be done, but from which no one can make a profit – and that we're running out of planet. These are not problems which capitalism can solve.

We need to get our heads around the fact that the employment experience is changing. For many people, retraining will be required more than once during their working life. Jobs for life already do not exist for many people. The idea that we do training at the start of adulthood followed by on-the-job experience has to go. It's not like that anymore. But capitalism is not well placed to accommodate or support non-linear career progressions or widespread job-switching across industries. Or job sharing or extended leisure time. We need a dynamic and forward-thinking, publicly-managed approach to lifelong learning and the active labour market. We also need public investment in education for its own sake, to enhance the quality of our lives and the legitimacy of our participatory democracy. This change in our attitudes to work will also entail a change in our attitudes to both education and leisure. Russell notes that some people object to any increase in leisure time on the grounds that the masses are not equipped to be able to handle so much spare time. He (correctly) adds that if this is in fact the case, then it's a shameful indictment on our society, and should be addressed without delay.[104]

The required transformation in the way we view work, and in the way we view the relationship between work and reward, is not limited to the idea of changing career patterns. We also need to accept that it's okay to work less. The response to automation and the advances of AI should be positive – relief at the prospect that there is less work that needs to be done. More time to spend with our loved ones, to pursue our interests, to learn things, to help people – to have time for ourselves and each other and to establish a meaningful work/life balance. But this response isn't possible while the dog-eat-dog capitalist labour market determines who has diamonds and who has doodley-squat – and ensures that almost everyone has the latter. (We shouldn't confuse the allocation of poverty and destitution by the labour market with the ridiculous notion that under capitalism rewards are intrinsically linked to effort. That is one of the fallacies we'll be dismantling in chapters 6 and 7.)

The concept of a post-work future has been gaining currency for many years and is often linked to proposals for a move towards a Universal Basic Income. I don't believe we can ever achieve a fully post-work society – or that we would actually want to, but I think we can get as close as we ought to and that we can get there relatively soon. My reservation about whether we really *want* to say goodbye to work doesn't spring from some moralistic attachment to the work ethic, but from the simple fact that some jobs need a human touch. I don't think we want our children's teachers or our parents' carers to be automatons, however good the AI gets.[105] Not so much *Fully Automated Luxury Communism*[106] as mainly automated, comfortable, post-capitalism. Not as catchy, as ambitious or as glamorous, but a more attainable goal, at least in the short term. I don't think that Universal Basic Income is the solution we're looking for either – not because it doesn't do the job of breaking – or at least weakening – the relationship between work and reward, between salary and survival, but because I think there's a structural approach which is preferable because it addresses the actual problem, not its symptoms. We'll look at that approach in Chapter 9.

3.5 The Changing Shape of Inequality

The second mechanism which could encourage large numbers of people to look beyond capitalism for answers is simply the fact that we have reached the point where improvements in the quality of life are not brought by ever greater consumption. Comprehensive research by Richard Wilkinson and Kate Pickett has shown that among developed countries the best quality of life is not a product of more wealth, but of less inequality. Not of the extent of capitalism, but of the extent of its mitigation.[107]

In developed countries we have enough stuff. Our lives will be improved by better distribution of work and resources – by less work, not by more bling. This approach to enriching lives by something other than endless consumption will also tackle problems in the developing world where there are more pressing needs than the manufacture of new varieties of disposable trainers to fend off cultural stagnation in the West.

Whether it's Sweden's steeply progressive tax rates or Japan's shallow earnings curve, countries with less inequality produce a better quality of life for their populations – right to the top of the income range. These countries deliver longer life expectancy, lower infant mortality, fewer suicides, decreased divorce rates, lower prison populations and so on.[108] Of course, these countries still exhibit capitalist economic structures, but these are the societies at the forefront of experiments with ways to mitigate the iniquity of capitalism. As such they're also the societies most likely to begin to move us away from capitalism altogether. In chapters 7-10 we'll go on to look at some suggestions for how this process might begin. Here we'll look at the changing nature and effects of inequality, which will help to illustrate why it's not possible to properly address this issue within a capitalist economic structure.

Thomas Piketty's thorough analysis of inequality in Europe and the US has revealed that 'Inequality with respect to capital is always greater than inequality with respect to labor. The distribution of capital ownership (and income from capital) is always more concentrated than the distribution of income from labor.'[109] This, he notes, is found in all countries, at all times (for which data is available), and the difference is always striking. In labour terms the bottom 50 per cent receive a quarter to a third of total labour income – approximately the same as the top 10 per cent. In terms of income from capital on the other hand, the bottom 50 per cent usually own nothing or almost nothing, while the top 10 per cent own between 50 and 90 per cent. This picture reinforces Marx's assessment that the important, defining characteristic of life under capitalism is not income, but ownership – or non-ownership – of capital. Joseph Stiglitz also notes huge inequalities in the US and places much of the blame for recent exacerbations of the trend on the power of the finance sector, arguing that 'Rents have moved dollars from the bottom and the middle to the top and distorted the market to the advantage of some and to the disadvantage of others.'[110] (Notice that here Stiglitz refers to *distortions* of the market, not the workings of the market. His point is that the logic of the market has been hijacked and undermined by rentiers, but – I would argue – such distortion is an inevitable consequence of the concentration of capital in the hands of a tiny minority. It's a feature of capitalism, not a bug.)

Stiglitz lists a number of changes to the tax system which he thinks would help to alleviate income inequality (closing loopholes and raising taxes for high earners, speculators and polluters) but recognises that the political and legal systems are set up to operate in favour of those with the deepest pockets.[111] Stiglitz and other leading economists who recognise that inequality is a blight on society tend to frame their solutions in terms of changes to the tax system. Those writing from a broadly Keynesian position might advocate – in addition to tax reform – government investment in public services. Economists favouring the heterodox approach known as *Modern Monetary Theory* might go further and offer more radical solutions such as a *jobs guarantee*, but none of these approaches deal with the fundamental, underlying issue, which is that most people do not exercise any form of control over any means of production, and as such must enter into unfavourable employment contracts in order to live any kind of dignified life. Stiglitz hints at this when he concedes that the natural resources of the US are 'resources that rightfully belong to *all* Americans'.[112] But in the same breath, he advocates dealing with this via higher taxes on the corporations who profit from those resources. If we really believe that natural resources *rightfully belong* to the community, then we need to start moving towards policies which really reflect that rightful ownership, rather than those which merely offer compensation for their appropriation. (In Chapter 6 we'll look at precedents for the 'compensation' approach in the work of theorists from Locke to Nozick, and at why such an approach is insufficient for addressing the problems we face.) While taxes will continue to play a role in national economies for a while yet, it's time to look beyond progressive taxation as a means of mitigating inequality. (Aside from anything else, as the effects of AI take hold in coming decades, there may be fewer and fewer people with an income to be taxed.) That's not to suggest that taxation has no role in moving us forward. In Chapter 9 we'll look at various approaches intended to progress us towards a more socialist footing, including Thomas Piketty's radical proposals to use the tax system to transform capitalism's concentrated and permanent resource ownership into a system of distributed temporary wealth.

One important role that taxation has played over the last 200 years is to introduce and reinforce the idea that those who benefit most from the way society is currently organised *ought* to be prepared to contribute more to its upkeep. This sentiment varies in strength from country to country, as well as across the political spectrum within each country. But in all modern, liberal democracies the idea that taxation is merely a form of theft and should be abolished is highly marginalised. Mainstream politicians may argue about how great the overall tax burden should be and how it should be distributed across different forms of taxation and different types of taxpayer, but no one seriously argues that it shouldn't exist. This is a start. This sentiment contains the seed of the idea that perhaps the particular distribution of wealth into which each of us was born was not the most equitable, or the fairest or one which bore much relation to the respective talents and efforts of the global population we became a new member of. It's almost as if there's an unspoken contract between those who are fabulously well-to-do and those who have doodley-squat: 'We'll contribute a chunk of tax so that you guys can have schools and hospitals and libraries and so on, if in return you don't ask too many questions about how come we seem to own the entire planet you just arrived on.' But now it's time to start asking those questions, and much of Chapter 6 does just that. Before we look at the moral and philosophical questions surrounding the transition away from capitalism, though, I'll provide some context with a very brief review of one aspect of the development of political ideology in the capitalist era in Chapter 4 and a discussion about the concept of equality in Chapter 5.

Part II
Ideology

4

Left and Right

Despite our best endeavours things seem to stay the same, the right keeps all the power and the left gets all the blame.
Flying Patrol Group, 1985[113]

Once we begin to view capitalism not only as an economic structure, but as part of a progression, rather than some kind of end-point, we can start to develop a better understanding of the politics of the bourgeois era, and of the possibilities of what might come next and how we might get there.

4.1 Origins

The most common taxonomy of political ideologies in the bourgeois era has been the familiar left-right spectrum. For generations this provided a standard reference point for politicians, commentators and the public – a common currency of political understanding. Since the 1950s this approach has come under increasing scrutiny with numerous alternative proposals either rejecting the left-right concept altogether, bending it into a horseshoe or adding new dimensions and axes.[114] It remains convenient shorthand in certain circumstances, but often causes confusion because what the terms mean has evolved over time, and the historical context has largely been forgotten. Despite the rise in identity-focused politics in recent years, the left-right axis is still most often perceived in an economic context – running from full-on *laissez-faire* free-market economics on the right to public ownership of essential services and major industries on the left. It's not the focus on the economic sphere that's the problem with this approach, but the attempt to align the concept of the political left with any particular *set of policies*. This just isn't possible once we take the historical context into account. The left now are clearly engaged in either mitigating the excesses of capitalism or replacing it altogether, but the entire concept of left and right in politics dates from the immediate aftermath of the French Revolution – a time when the left were the advocates of capitalism – pursuing revolutionary change to overturn feudal privilege. The original left[115] during the revolutionary period in France drew support from many factions opposed to the *Ancien Régime*. Peasants and labourers yes – but also merchants and early industrialists, the emerging capitalist class, or *bourgeoisie*. The left, in its opposition to the 'old order', demanded an end to a wide range of injustices, and while its successes benefitted almost everyone outside of the old alliance of monarchy, nobility and clergy, the real winners were the emerging bourgeoisie. It was the bourgeois interest who came to dominate political life, bringing laws and institutions into line with their capitalist ambitions. Given this historical background, the concept of the political left cannot be seen as inherently antagonistic to capitalism or identified with a given set of policies, but rather should apply to a direction of travel. The only way to reconcile the pro-capitalist origins of the concept of the political left with its current anti-capitalist incarnation is to see it as a programme advocating the progressive ideas of the Enlightenment, adapting to historical circumstances and advancing from tradition to modernity – from superstition and fear to rationality and understanding. (Despite accusations of – and flirtations with – post-modernism, the left is firmly a modernist project.) From this perspective, some degree of ideological continuity can be detected between capitalism and socialism, as consecutive stages on the road from religiously justified feudal hierarchy to secular demands for equality.

The change that the left were then demanding was an end

to feudalism – the removal of various social, political and cultural institutions which had frustrated capitalist ambitions. The emerging bourgeoisie – in revolutionary France as in seventeenth-century England – had found their progress hampered by arbitrary justice, favours, prerogatives, customary rights and obligations and different sets of laws for different social classes. In order to flourish, capitalism needs certainty and predictability. Laws need to be codified and to apply across the board. Investors need to know in advance that if their commercial judgement is correct, then they'll be rewarded with the proceeds, not see their effort and investment handed over to court favourites by a monarch ruling by arbitrary judgement. Monarchs had enjoyed near absolute, God-given authority which had been legitimised over centuries through doctrines of *Divine Right* and the *Great Chain of Being*. Limiting their power wasn't just a case of developing superior economic arrangements and better technology, or of seizing political power. An ingrained belief system had to be broken down and – equally – something had to replace it. The emerging capitalist order needed an ideological legitimacy.

That legitimacy was provided by the philosophers of the Enlightenment – Locke's justification of private property, Paine's rights of man, Wollstonecraft's rights of women, de Tocqueville's democracy and later the utilitarianism of Jeremy Bentham and John Stuart Mill (embodied in the concept of 'the greatest happiness for the greatest number'). The philosophies of all of these thinkers include a requirement of egalitarianism in that they treat all men's interests (and for some of them, even all women's interests) as being of equal value regardless of wealth or station – in a certain set of specifically limited ways, no one man's needs are considered more important than those of others on the grounds of their social standing. These thinkers developed the concept of rights based not on hereditary privilege, but on no more than the simple fact of being a person. This, in turn, inspired the formulation in the US *Declaration of Independence* that 'all men are created equal...with certain unalienable Rights'.[116] The text of the *Declaration* omitted women, and the historical context plainly excludes many actually existing men from the rhetorical construct 'all men' on the grounds of class and race, but it was a start. The philosophical underpinning of capitalism and its emphasis on rights attached to the status of being a human could only lead in one direction and over time Western-liberal democracies began to recognise that people counted as humans even if they were not wealthy white men. From eighteenth-century abolitionists and nineteenth-century radicals, through the Chartists, the Reform League and Suffragettes to the UN Declaration of Human Rights, the civil rights movement in the US and the anti-apartheid campaigns of the 1980s the doctrine that people have a value solely by virtue of being people – and that there's something intrinsically equal about each person's value – has become an integral part of the fabric of political ideology in the capitalist era. Although *really-existing capitalism* has often failed to deliver on these ideals, we shouldn't ignore areas where progress has been made. Since universal adult suffrage in 1928, in the UK we've had the Equal Pay Act (1970), the Sex Discrimination Act (1975), the Race Relations Act (1976), the Disability Discrimination Act (1995) – all eventually consolidated into the Equalities Act in 2010. In many countries much more is being done. Of course there is still a long way to go, particularly in moving on from legislative instruments to actual equality, but that shouldn't detract from the direction of travel of the past few hundred years. Political power in capitalist countries is fundamentally legitimised through the concept of democratic consent, based on equality before the law and the principle (if not the practice) of one vote of equal value for every adult human. And yet discrimination on the basis of race and gender still persists – and not just in the occasional encounter with citizens who didn't get the memo, but in patterns embedded in the fabric of Western society and its institutions.[117]

4.2 The Duality of the Left

In terms of contemporary politics, this helps to explain some of the confusion of what it means to be considered 'left-wing'. In both the UK and the US there is a palpable tension between the socialist left (mainly focusing on economics) and the liberal left (mainly concerned with identity politics). The opposition to Trump was demonstrably weakened by its division into factions coming from very different philosophical positions. In the UK the leadership of the Labour Party (under Starmer at the time of writing) spends more time attacking its own left-wing than scrutinising what is probably the most incompetent and corrupt UK government in living memory. Jeremy Gilbert has observed that the dividing line in British society between those who want to see decisive, structural change to improve the lives of all of us (and in particular the least well off) and those who do not want to see such change currently runs right through the Labour Party.[118] From the Parliamentary Labour Party and the party machine to the membership and potential members – in different proportions for each of those groups there are those in the Labour movement who want structural change and those who do not. This line is the dividing line between the liberal left, who think capitalism can be reformed, and the socialist left, who recognise that capitalism has to go.

The core, driving theme of liberal identity politics is to point out the hypocrisy of the existing system – **to call out the hypocrisy of capitalist liberal democracy in failing to live up to its own principles.** Essentially, the liberal complaint is that modern Western capitalism fails to deliver the fundamental freedoms upon which its own philosophical legitimacy relies. We can call these *bourgeois freedoms,* not in the pejorative sense of 'freedoms enjoyed by the bourgeoisie' but in the simply descriptive sense of 'freedoms won in the bourgeois era'. Whatever is wrong with capitalism it has some advantages over feudalism and the acceptance that all humans have a right to these freedoms is one of them – and the liberal complaint is that really-existing capitalism fails to fulfil this philosophical ambition.

In contrast, the thrust of the socialist left (including the democratic-socialist left) is to argue that **the bourgeois freedoms of liberal capitalism are insufficient to deliver real freedom** to the mass of humanity. For the socialist left, the demands of the great bourgeois upheavals – the French Revolution, the English Civil Wars and the Glorious Revolution of 1688 – are welcome, but don't go far enough. It's great that people gained (theoretical) equality before the law, and – eventually – a vote each in a participatory democracy, but it's the unequal distribution of wealth, income and opportunity that's really holding society back.

There is no necessary requirement to abolish capitalism in the liberal movement demanding that human and civil rights are delivered. These are not socialist demands, but they do illustrate a continuity between capitalism and socialism. Both projects demand an equality of *something*. Socialism demands all the equalities promoted (if not delivered) by capitalist ideology and more. In Chapter 5 we'll address Amartya Sen's famous question aimed at egalitarian liberal capitalists, *Equality of What?* We'll note how discussions of equality within a capitalist mindset hit a brick wall when it comes to the proposition that a formal recognition of rights is not sufficient – that without the material means to access the actual benefits of rights, any formal right is somewhat meaningless. The only real way to address this problem is to ensure that all people enjoy sufficient material wellbeing to enable their formal rights to have real meaning. The problem here, though, is that although capitalist ideology is founded on the idea of natural rights, it also embodies the premise that property rights are not only natural, but also that they trump any other rights. Property rights attain this **protected moral status** via an ideological sleight of hand in which infractions upon property are taken to be infractions upon individual freedom, itself the greatest sin in the capitalist world. This idea holds such sway that arguments in favour of material equalities can be summarily brushed aside and – as we'll see – even proposals for universal *sufficiency* receive short shrift from capitalist philosophers. Such is the morally protected status of private property rights that even the right to life cannot compete.

So the main difference between the liberal left and the socialist leftis that the former calls out capitalism for not living up to its own standards while the latter argues that those standards would be insufficient, even if they were met. In terms of today's choices, the socialist left takes all of the rights and demands of the liberal left and *adds* to them, to root out economic disadvantage too. The liberal left has little reciprocal interest in adding socialist objectives to its agenda.

There is, though, one area where the liberal demands cross into socialist territory, and that is in the recognition that *given the course of history and the details of our route to the present* there is a case for demanding more than equality before the law and equality of political participation. The history of past injustices has an influence on current society which any reasonable concept of justice would address. Affirmative action policies in the US and women-only short lists in the UK[119]are examples of policies based on this common ground – the acceptance that the legacy of historical discrimination, and the continued existence of inequality means that formal equality of treatment and status is not a sufficient condition for justice in really-existing modern capitalism.

Most people who would consider their politics to be left-leaning would recognise elements of both the socialist and liberal philosophical positions in their own ideological make-up. The numbers perceiving themselves as belonging firmly to one strand and viewing the other as part of the problem have probably increased in recent years in both the UK and the US.

4.3 The Duality of the Right

A similar duality can be seen on the right, though as always, they seem to be better at living with their differences for their mutual benefit. In this case, the difference is probably more easily observable in the UK than the US. On the one hand there are those who appear to regret the passing of feudalism – Jacob Rees-Mogg springs unpleasantly to mind. There is a large slice of right-wing thought in Britain that feeds on faux nostalgia about the Empire and draws emotional strength from ridiculous, anachronistic traditions – the monarchy, fox-hunting, everything about daily life at Westminster and so on. While these Tories look to the likes of Roger Scruton for philosophical justification of their nostalgia, there's also a faction of support for the modern, ruthless, free-market economics of F.A. Hayek[120] and the (supposedly) clinical political philosophy of Robert Nozick[121]. Of course, these two factions share considerable common ground and to different degrees co-exist within most people on the right – their differences more of emphasis than argument, of style more than substance. While pining for days of landed abstention from anything as vulgar as going to work, the old Tories have to accept that tradition and hierarchy don't pay the bills and as such they must rely for their continued status and privilege on neoliberal economic policies. For their part, the bankers and industrialists know deep down that the truly meritocratic free market they like to talk of in the abstract would in reality be a cut-throat world forcing them to compete without the leg-up from the right school and the security of the old-boys network, and this is a prospect that keeps them just sweet enough to maintain a respect for the traditional hierarchies of social status.

So we can see a continuum encompassing mainstream politics, with four overlapping approaches. From right to left we have the Tories regretting the passing of feudalism, but broadly content with the privilege they retain under capitalism, then the right-libertarians – enthusiastic about capitalism and its bounties, but not so committed to its philosophical underpinnings as to want the inconvenience of a level playing field. Next up there are the liberals, holding capitalism to its word and demanding equality before the law regardless of a person's identity (or their self-identity) but also aware that no one's life is an abstract concept – that we've all arrived on the planet in a historical context and that there may be some hangovers from the past which need redressing. Finally, at the leftward end of this mainstream continuum we have various flavours of socialism, which share the liberal conviction that people's present situation is largely a product of the past they find themselves born into, and that a valid political programme might include plans to minimise the upshot of those historical circumstances. Socialists, though, push further than the liberal demands of redress for generations of cultural and social discrimination – for really-existing capitalism's failure to live up to the ideological principles upon which it was built. Socialists demand redress, not only for capitalism's inability to deliver what it promises, but for the consequences of capitalism's successes. Capitalism, as we have seen in Chapter 2, delivers propertylessness to the mass of the population, and socialists argue that this is a situation which requires correction – either by mitigation of capitalist excesses, or by wholesale replacement of the capitalist system itself.

As we've noted, the birth of capitalism was accompanied by – and legitimised by – an insistence that in some way, on some measure, there is something (in theory, if not always in practice) which people are entitled to an equal amount of, solely on the basis of being people. This entity, which capitalist ideology insists we must all enjoy to an equal extent, is often expressed in popular discourse as *equality before the law*. In more philosophical tracts it is sometimes referred to as *self-ownership*. Such is the prevalence of this idea in modern capitalist societies that it's easy to forget that for most of human history the ownership of people and their capacities was not distributed equally among populations. In slave societies a slave-owner may own many people, and slaves own no one, not even themselves. Whereas under capitalism we each enjoy ownership rights over exactly one person (ourselves), in pre-capitalist societies this was not the case. Some who write from a historical materialist perspective further divide pre-capitalist society broadly into slave-based economic structures and a range of post-slavery economic structures (broadly lumped together as feudalism) in which most people are granted ownership of their own person, but do not own all of their own labour power – some of which is owned by their feudal 'superior'.

Uneven distribution of personal freedom was a central feature of pre-capitalist economic structures and remains a feature of modern non-capitalist countries which attracts condemnation from across the political spectrum of the capitalist world (though not enough to do without the profits from slave labour – let's not get carried away with capitalism's commitment to this, it's most fundamental concept). The point here is that the equalising instinct – the tendency towards egalitarianism – is not an anti-capitalist ideological ambition. The difference between capitalist ideology and socialist ideology is not that one favours equality and the other doesn't, but what kind and extent of equality each requires. Jerry Cohen describes egalitarianism as the idea that, 'There is something which justice requires people to have equal amounts of...not "no matter what", but to whatever extent is allowed by values which compete with distributive equality.'[122] As long as egalitarianism itself is perceived as an anti-capitalist position, defenders of capitalism will continue to trot out caricatures of the egalitarian spirit as utopian fantasy doomed to end in absurd excess[123]. Once we recognise that capitalism itself requires (ideologically speaking) some form of equality, then the conversation changes from a discussion of the virtues or otherwise of the process of equalisation, and has to address what it is that is being equalised, how far we should go, and what competing values might need to be considered. Supporters of capitalism cannot argue that the pursuit of egalitarian aims is in itself unjust or unnecessary, since, as we've shown, capitalism itself relies on equality of *something*. Instead, they must explain why the egalitarian impulse is desirable and justified to the extent that it suits them, but undesirable and unjustified in cases where it might suit others. What does equality before the law have, which equality of opportunity, or equality of wealth or income do not have?

4.4 Civil Rights and Natural Rights

We've noted above that the US *Declaration of Independence* asserts that 'all men are created equal...with certain unalienable Rights'. The first article of the French *Declaration of the Rights of Man and of the Citizen* similarly asserts that 'Men are born and remain free and equal in rights.'[124] These declarations of bourgeois consciousness are not awarding rights to anyone, but recognising that they already exist, that they are a product of nature and not subject to human whim. Such is the strength of these ideas that it's now almost impossible to imagine a world in which they were new and controversial. But in pre-capitalist Europe rights were attached to social status, and were by no means equally distributed. Debates over the question of rights came to a head more than a century before the US and French *Declarations,* during the English Civil Wars and particularly during the 'Putney Debates' in 1647 – in the interbellum period between the first and second wars. At the end of the first war a split emerged within the parliamentarian New Model Army. Cromwell and the army *Grandees* took a conciliatory approach to negotiations with Charles I, but groups such as the Levellers, Ranters and Diggers were emerging at this time, gaining support among the ranks and demanding a radical new society.[125] The radicals were allowed to put their case over 2 weeks of debate in Putney, now part of south-west London. Although the discussions were inconclusive[126] they illustrate the wrangling over the source and nature of rights, and the novelty of the ideas at the time. Reading the minutes – which were only discovered in 1890 – there's a clear sense that the protagonists are feeling their way through unchartered territory.[127] These were not like the tired and well-rehearsed debates we've become used to seeing our politicians engage in. The Levellers advocated parliamentary sovereignty and universal male suffrage with Thomas Rainsborough arguing that, 'The poorest he that is in England has a life to live as the greatest he; and therefore truly sir I think it's clear that every man that is to live under a government ought first by his own consent to put himself under that government.'[128] Rainsborough's reference to England is important here as it aligns with the Leveller's common assertions of the rights of 'freeborn Englishmen'. These are civil rights accorded to those who have the status of Englishmen, not natural rights which are enjoyed by virtue of being a human male. (Though some radical groups already supported the idea that natural rights might apply to women too it would be a long time before such a view became widespread.) Henry Ireton, Cromwell's son-in-law – representing the leadership – glosses over the distinction between natural and civil rights and counters that property ownership should be the basis of the electoral franchise. He cites the conventional view that only a stakeholder will really have the interests of the country at heart whereas those who 'have no permanent interest in the state, [but] whatever interest he hath he may carry about with him' have no stake in society, since they could easily move to another kingdom.[129] Ireton presents his case, not only as the conventional practice embedded in the constitution, but also as the obvious pragmatic solution. It's framed in terms of interests and who is best placed to make judgements, not on some new-fangled idea of *rights*, whether derived from the state of nature or the fact of being English-born. Where would it end – all this talk of rights? Ireton sees that the logic of equal rights, whatever their foundation, is ultimately incompatible with the institution of private property: 'Is it by the right of nature? (whatever it be) that you pretend, by which you can say, one man hath an equal right with another to the choosing of him that shall govern him – by the same right of nature, he hath the same [equal] rights in any goods he sees – meat, drink, clothes – to take and use them for his sustenance.'[130] Ireton was not accusing the agitators of wanting to do away with property but warning them that such abolition would be the logical conclusion of their attempt to introduce principles of equal rights. Although Rainsborough supported the concept of property, when he argued that 'my person it is more dear than my estate,'[131] he was clearly suggesting that people are more important than property – a situation which Ireton recognised as fatal to the concept of private property. (If *A* owns all the land and chooses not to deal with *B*, the institution of private property upholds *A*'s property rights over *B*'s right not to die of starvation. To assert *B*'s right to life would require *A* to surrender some degree of control over their property.) The debates were left hanging in November 1647 when the king escaped and was reunited with royalist forces. A second war now loomed, and there was to be no time for discussions on the future constitution. Cromwell, clearly rattled by the radical ideas and the extent of their support, turned to violent suppression, effectively putting an end to the Leveller cause by 1649. The ideas didn't go away, though, and somehow the circle would need to be squared. How could the promotion of equal rights be reconciled with the practical necessity to overlook even the right to life, in the event that it might conflict with the right to own property? Rather than getting to the bottom of this conundrum, a sleight of hand was devised, largely by John Locke in the late seventeenth century, upon which an entire bourgeois ideology was built, complete with misdirections, contradictions and *Declarations* – of rights and of independence.

In Chapter 6 we'll dissect Locke's illusions and those of his philosophical descendants, but first we should address the question of equality itself, and consider candidates for what it is that should be equalised and what competing values might limit the extent to which equalisation is justifiable or desirable. We have already noted (see Chapter 3) that inequality is damaging to both quality of life and to progress, and now we should turn our attention to what kind of equality we should be promoting (if any), and what other values might restrict the scope of our egalitarian ambition.

5

Equality of What?

> *...the majestic equality of the law, which forbids the rich as well as the poor to sleep under bridges, to beg in the streets and to steal bread*
>
> Anatole France, 1894[132]

G.A. Cohen argues that the purpose of egalitarianism is 'to eliminate involuntary disadvantage'[133] and – as we've noted in Chapter 4 – a fundamental thesis of bourgeois ideology is that this principle should be applied to people's legal status and their participation in the political system. These measures of *equality before the law* and *equal political participation* set bourgeois ideology apart from life under pre-capitalist economic structures and have become cornerstones of the bourgeois worldview, even though *really-existing capitalism* frequently fails to deliver them in practice.

Should we go further, though, and promote the application of the egalitarian principle to other areas of life? In his 1979 Tanner Lecture, Amartya Sen posed the question *Equality of What?*[134] Sen sought to identify the fundamental currency of equality – not the evidence or symptoms of equality but the aspects of life which egalitarians should seek to distribute equally (or at least *less unequally*) among the population. Before we look at some of the candidates for the answer to Sen's question, we should ask what it is that motivates the egalitarian principle. The Enlightenment thinkers who founded and developed the bourgeois principles of equality before the law and equality of social status were clear on the purpose of this ideological commitment – the motivation for this move to greater equality was the promotion of justice.[135] If we accept this approach – that greater equality leads in some instances to more justice, and I can see no reason not to – then those arguing against extensions of the egalitarian principle into new aspects of the human experience must take this into account. They must be prepared to defend their opposition to extensions of equality on the grounds that either:

a. the extension of equality in question does not increase justice (while maintaining that the historical delivery of bourgeois equality *did* increase justice), or
b. some other benefits, which outweigh an increase in justice, are threatened by the suggested extension of equality.

What this means is that in the absence of evidence to the contrary, we should assume that any extension of equality represents an extension of justice. The currently dominant assumption – that moves to greater equality must be justified – needs to be turned upside-down – it is resistance to such moves which needs to be justified.

We should bear in mind this general desirability of the egalitarian principle (all other things being equal) as we now examine some of the potential answers to Sen's question 'equality of what?' Sen turns first to John Rawls who provided a major advance over the utilitarian approach in his 1971 *A Theory of Justice*. Recall that the utilitarian maxim 'the greatest happiness for the greatest number' treats all individuals as equals but seeks to *maximise* 'happiness' rather than to equalise it. While Rawls' ideal society might tolerate inequalities, he envisions institutions which seek to promote an egalitarian, rather than a maximising, distribution, and the thing to be distributed is not some vague sense of 'happiness' or 'utility' but what he termed 'public goods'. By this he means 'things that every rational man is presumed to want,' including 'rights, liberties and opportunities, income and wealth, and the social bases of self-respect'.[136] The distribution of these, he argued, should ideally be more equal than is currently the case (inequalities must be justified on the criteria that they make the least well off, better off), but he does not place egalitarianism at the top of his agenda – moves towards greater equality must take second place to considerations of liberty. This is an important restriction which we'll return to later in this chapter, and at length in Chapter 6.

Sen himself moves the argument on again to combine the distribution of public goods favoured by Rawls with the 'happiness' at the centre of utilitarian theories, to arrive at a concern with 'what goods *do* to human beings'. Cohen refers to Sen's stance as a promotion of something more than either goods or happiness but a kind of 'nutrition' produced by the right quantities of each.[137]

The problem with these discussions about what should be the currency of egalitarian ambitions is that they skirt around the issue of how those ambitions might actually be achieved. I don't mean questions of how we might measure happiness or how we could distribute self-respect equally (though those are thorny issues), I mean that these approaches don't take into account the elephant in the room – that formal equalities don't necessarily translate into actual equalities. The absence of a formal barrier to liberty or opportunity or utility does not render that goal attainable to those with insufficient resources to reach it. In the end, equality of anything requires some degree of equality of resources – of wealth. The concentration of wealth into ever fewer hands confounds any attempt to construct a meaningfully egalitarian distribution of any other value. And it is proposals to redistribute ownership of resources in pursuit of egalitarian ambition which meet the greatest resistance. Our challenge is to present the case for egalitarian redistribution in such a way as to make the transition realistically possible. *How* we might begin to practically move towards that situation is discussed in Chapter 9, but first we must conclude our discussion of *why* we should move to that situation. One part of that task involves illustrating that a more equitable distribution of resource ownership represents a fair and just ambition – some objections to which will be addressed in Chapter 6. The other main part of the task involves demonstrating that most people in the world would be better off (or at least no worse off) under a more equitable system – and it is that claim to which we now turn.

5.1 Wealth Inequality

The benefits of a more equitable distribution of resources are not limited to the enjoyment of a healthier bank-balance, or a lower overdraft, or a better quality of material life – a nicer house, a healthier diet, more things…At the top of this chapter we used the term 'bourgeois equality' to describe equality before the law and equality of access to political participation – two essential features of capitalist ideology. In practice, access to those rights is clearly greater for those with considerable material wealth. No one seriously doubts that wealth allows access to levels of legal justice and political influence beyond that available to most citizens in liberal democracies, or that poverty reduces such access[138]. If the equalisation of political participation is desirable (bourgeois ideology says that it is), and the connection between wealth and political influence is inevitable, then the bourgeois goal of equalising political power *requires* at least a desire towards a greater equalisation of wealth – yet the bourgeoisie, on the whole, seem to exhibit no such desire. Now, there may be objections to such an equalisation on other grounds, but in the conversation about the pros and cons of wealth-equalising policies, the omission of the influence of wealth on access to political influence would be a serious deficiency. Supporters of capitalism cannot reasonably defend the legal and political privilege which wealth can buy because their own ideological standpoint revolves around a doctrine of equality of access to these facilities. Yet the promotion of the kind of resource redistribution which would enable genuine equality in these fields meets numerous objections from the bourgeois interest.

5.2 *The Cult of the Status Quo*

Thomas Nagel suggests in *Equality and Partiality* that humankind is stuck in limbo, unable to reconcile the needs of the community for fairness with the needs of the individual for liberty – to do 'justice to the equal importance of all persons without making unacceptable demands on individuals'.[139] Nagel argues that the demands of the poor for a greater share of resources are reasonable claims, but no more so than the claims of the wealthy for the right to hang on to the disproportionate share of resources they currently control. He concludes, not only that we do not have the tools to envisage a solution to this dilemma but also that such a solution might not exist. The problem with Nagel's approach is that it gives the status quo undue reverence and in doing so it favours inaction – and accepts existing inequalities. Even if Nagel's point is only supposed to hold water in modern, Western, capitalist, liberal democracies, the status quo – from which he argues that the wealthy are justified in resisting deviation – is a pretty diverse collection of situations across numerous societies. Yet the upshot of this type of argument is always 'that's far enough'.[140] Whether we are considering a relatively less unequal society (such as pre-Thatcher Britain[141]) or a far more unequal society (such as Trump's US[142]) Nagel's 'solution' is to do nothing. That Nagel's approach requires us to deem as reasonable the wishes of the wealthy to maintain the status quo – whatever it may be – gives it the air of a strained attempt to justify inequality, *whatever its extent and however it may have arisen*.

The Rawlsian approach discussed above suffers from the same deficiency. Whatever the current situation, and however it arose, almost any redistribution of public goods at all can be deemed a 'loss of liberty' for someone. In the end, Rawls' concern to limit any adjustments to those not affecting anyone's current lifestyle favours those who already enjoy a generous allocation of resources. In addition to discouraging change, this undue reverence inadvertently accorded to the status quo by both Rawls and Nagel provides unwarranted ideological legitimacy for both the current distribution of resources and the historical processes by which it arose. By limiting our options to those which respect current distributions – whether or not those distributions were arrived at by unjust means – we would effectively be accepting the weak and circular argument that we should not seek to redistribute resources simply because the current distribution already exists. The question of the legitimacy of actually existing property distributions receives more attention in Chapter 6.

5.3 *Equality or Sufficiency?*

Harry Frankfurt takes a different line, arguing that people who oppose inequality are often confused about what it is they object to – what they really object to (he obligingly informs them) is poverty. What they ought really to want then, he concludes, is not less inequality, but more *sufficiency*.[143] If a person has sufficient goods and rights and whatever else they need, he argues, it shouldn't be relevant to them, or to us, how much wealth someone else has.

The obvious problem with this approach is that there is no objective measure of sufficiency. If person *A* has *x* goods and person *B* has half *x*, then between them they have 1.5*x* and a switch to equality would leave them with 0.75*x* each. Any objection by *A* to such equality is motivated by their opinion that 0.75*x* is insufficient for their own needs, while also relying on their commitment to the idea that 0.5*x* is sufficient for person *B*'s needs. It's not difficult to see that *A*'s position is motivated by self-interest, rather than any kind of objective logic. While the egalitarian approach ensures that the level of wealth with which we expect others to be satisfied is no less than the level we expect for ourselves, the subjective nature of what constitutes sufficiency contains no such guard against self-interest masquerading as philosophical justification.

Sufficiency for all is, of course, preferable to our current global situation where millions live with – and die because of – insufficient resources. Supporters of capitalism, though, argue that poverty should be addressed not by sharing wealth more equally, but by creating more wealth. They argue that egalitarian concerns inhibit productive development and thus constitute the biggest threat to eliminating insufficiency or poverty. Although capitalism may not eliminate or even mitigate huge inequalities, they argue, its unique capacity to increase productive output means that more people are rescued from poverty and toil under capitalism's inequality than would be the case under a seemingly more just, but less productively efficient, alternative. The claim is that even those at the bottom are better off under capitalist inequality than they would be under egalitarian inefficiency. In short, those with the least will benefit more from a small share of a bigger pie, than from an equal share of a smaller pie. This argument relies not only on ambitions for the future size and distribution of the pie for which there is absolutely no historical justification, but also on the idea that capitalism is – and always will be – the system most suited to the satisfaction of human needs. The errors in this approach have already been addressed in Chapter 3.

Capitalism has an excellent track record of increasing productive capacity and extending sufficiency to greater numbers – though not necessarily to a greater proportion of humankind. That capitalism is uniquely suited to produce the abundance required for us to realise our potential is one of a limited number of points upon which both Marx and twenty-first century capitalists agree. The difference is that for Marx capitalism cannot deliver the freedom its productive capacity makes possible – for capitalists, capitalism *is* the freedom it makes possible. This difference of opinion is largely due to different approaches to the concept of freedom, which is the subject of the next chapter, but first we should consider another objection to the egalitarian approach – the claim that inequality is a necessary *and inevitable* part of the human experience.

5.4 Is Inequality Inevitable?

At the start of this chapter I argued that – since capitalist ideology is founded on one type of equality, and since the motivation for that egalitarian impulse is the promotion of justice – then other types of equality should not be ruled out without good reason and fair consideration, as it's not unreasonable to attach to them a potential to increase justice. Blithe comments about human nature and how equality is a nice idea that can't work in practice are not sufficient to reject an egalitarian approach. In the pre-capitalist era, doctrines such as the *Divine Right of Kings* and the *Great Chain of Being* led to assumptions that human nature would cause a descent into the abyss if the bourgeois ideals of equality before the law or equality of political participation were adopted. Just as early proponents of capitalism were right in thinking that human nature was more adaptable than their feudal critics thought, it's likely that human nature is flexible enough to manage in a world where wealth is not concentrated in the bank accounts of a handful of families. As for appeals to the historical record for evidence that egalitarianism and success are incompatible – any such claim fails on the grounds that most 'successful' countries are more egalitarian now than they were *x* number of years ago, whatever the value of *x* and under any reasonable definition of 'successful'. It's significant that the UK and US – home to many of the most vociferous supporters of the idea that egalitarianism is to blame for economic stagnation and decline – are the very economies struggling to maintain the growth of past decades, despite increasing inequality. Thomas Piketty shows that inequality is not a necessary price of development, progress and growth by comparing the relatively high inequality and moderate growth of the *Belle Époque* (1880-1914) with the far lower inequality of the period from 1930-1980 which corresponded to 'some of the strongest growth ever observed'.[144] The high marginal tax rates he recommends (60-70 per cent for those enjoying greater than 10x the average wealth or income and 80-90 per cent for those exceeding 100x the average) are consistent with the rates in the UK and US during this latter period of robust growth.

The musings of celebrity psychologist and YouTube star Jordan Peterson shouldn't have any bearing on a serious discussion but the widespread dissemination of his approach to this question can't really be ignored, so I'll quickly address it here. Peterson argues that inequality is an inevitable feature of the human condition. (He also – bizarrely – argues that Marx misattributes inequality to capitalism[145], ignoring at least tens of thousands of words Marx wrote about slavery and feudalism[146] – but then he also admits to hardly having read anything by Marx[147], so his lack of understanding is understandable.) As evidence for the inevitability of inequality Peterson equates human existence to the game of Monopoly and triumphantly declares that however many times you play the game, 'someone always ends up with all the damn money'.[148] He says this is 'the inevitable consequence of multiple trades that are conducted randomly'. He asserts this as if he's revealing some profound logic, but in fact the phenomenon is actually no more than the inevitable consequence of the rules of Monopoly stating that the game doesn't end till one person has all the money. He makes a similarly nonsensical claim about a coin-toss trading game: if you keep playing till one person ends up with all the money, one person will always end up with all the money! He extrapolates from this a fundamental law of human existence that we all just have to put up with: however much we object to millions of deaths through starvation every year, in a world where a quarter of our food goes to waste, there's absolutely nothing we can do about it...[149]

As if the Monopoly and coin-flip analogies were not enough, Peterson (in the same lecture) has some sciency stuff to explain the inevitability of inequality. He recruits the Pareto Principle, which he variously characterises as the 80/20 rule or the more academic sounding (but still entirely wrong) idea that in almost any situation, 'The square root of the number of people under consideration have half of the volume of what's under consideration.' And he goes on to make an extraordinary claim for it: 'It's a feature of every single system of production that we know of, no matter who set it up and how it operates...and we don't know what to do about that.' This bizarre claim entails that the wealth distribution in twentieth-century America matched that in third-century Borneo and ninth-century Sicily and twenty-first century Scotland – and everywhere else, at all times in history.His claim isn't true in any of those cases, or in the global economy today, for which it is wrong by a mile – by a factor of several hundred. But Peterson's absurd claim is not only that this distribution happens in every country on earth – and in all countries between them – all the time, it's even more than that. He claims that it's inevitable and that there's nothing we can do about it! It's not all bad news, from Planet Peterson, though. We shouldn't worry about economic inequality, he argues, because the problem with not having any money is not the lack of money. He justifies this with an 'anecdote' about a guy who got himself into trouble when he had some money. Really? Are we going to base our approach to global poverty on the patronising notion that if poor people have money, they're just going to get into trouble with it?[150]

Peterson makes another claim against the egalitarian motive. In response to claims that the opportunities provided by formal bourgeois equalities don't always deliver real equality he warns against trying to engineer outcomes, stating that 'equality of outcome considerations are detestable and dangerous beyond belief'.[151] Despite the evidence of progressive taxation systems, the NHS in the UK, welfare safety nets and so on, Peterson tends to view anything more egalitarian than formal bourgeois equality as the start of the slippery slope to the gulags but this approach lacks any kind of subtlety or nuance – or any supporting empirical evidence.

Peterson's views are not dissimilar to the Victorian dichotomy of the deserving and undeserving poor – those who scrape by without any assistance deserve some help, but don't need it, and those who struggle to get by need some help but don't deserve it. However, if we dismount the moral high-horse and just try to work out the best way to think about this problem we can easily see that people are differently able to convert opportunities into outcomes and that there are different types of inhibitors to that process of conversion. Rather than assuming that people are poor converters because they are lazy, feckless wastrels, we might ask whether it's because they lack the required skills, education, training or talents. In some cases, that's something they can do something about, in other cases it isn't. In some cases it's something we, the wider society, can do something about – by providing better educational opportunities, better training facilities and so on. In some cases, poor conversion abilities are insurmountable, and must be compensated for by wider society. It's important to note that the particular skills or talents required to be a successful converter of opportunities into positive outcomes aren't fixed features of the human condition. They are almost entirely context-dependent. Medieval Belgium had little use for the exceptional talents of George Best or David Attenborough, for example, in much the same way that expert type-cutters and pearl-divers might struggle to find any demand for their talents in twenty-first century Wolverhampton. Different careers are differently rewarded under capitalism on the basis of their market value which is usually not a good reflection of their value to society. (We'll look in more detail at this phenomenon in chapters 6 and 8.) Nor is the market allocation of people to well-rewarded careers a true reflection of their skills and abilities – the higher echelons of most professions are populated largely by the children of well-to-do parents. Despite the ideological commitment of the bourgeoisie to the concept of meritocracy, it's rare to find their children anywhere near a level playing field.

The differential abilities of people to convert opportunities into outcomes is sometimes used by capitalists as evidence that inequality is an inevitable feature of the human condition, but we have mechanisms in place which exacerbate this issue – there's no reason they cannot be exchanged for mechanisms to mitigate it. The observation that humans are differently able to convert resources into outcomes is not a false one, but it does not follow that current levels of inequality are inevitable. The observed fact can't carry the conceptual weight that anti-egalitarian ideology places on it.

Finally in this chapter, a short note on the concept of 'levelling-up'. There's a notion implicit in discussions surrounding redistribution of resources that the problem with egalitarianism is that the wealthy would inevitably face a reduction in their standard of living, because any such redistribution would necessarily see resources currently under their control transferred to others. A further, often unspoken implication of this idea is that the well-off would have no objection to a situation of equalised wealth, if that was brought about by some miracle of new production allowing everyone access to untold riches, rather than a transfer of assets from the wealthy to the poor. In fact, though, such a scenario would have a considerable impact on the lives of the well-off. One of the hallmarks of a wealthy lifestyle is not having to do everything for yourself – employing cleaners, gardeners, drivers, nannies, maids, personal assistants etc. If everyone had as much wealth as the currently wealthy, then no one would need to work in those occupations, and the wealthy lifestyle would lose most of its comfort and much of its appeal. Perhaps the opposition to equality might actually be influenced as much by the loss of inequality as by the loss of property itself. For wealthy opponents of egalitarianism, it's not necessarily enough for them to remain wealthy – the lifestyles to which they have become accustomed also require the poor to remain poor.

In this chapter, we've established that – even from the standpoint of bourgeois ideology – egalitarian motives should not be rejected without compelling grounds. We've considered the question of what it is that there ought to be equal amounts of – and observed that unless utility or public goods or self-respect or anything else is accompanied by the resources to actually realise their benefits, then the absence of formal barriers to them doesn't necessarily count for much. Without sufficient resources to exercise them, formal freedoms are hollow promises.

We've examined the resistance to the equalisation of resources for various reasons and found the sufficiency argument to be logically lacking and the inevitability argument to be based on faulty reasoning. We've noted an attachment to the status quo which betrays a resistance to change based on self-interest rather than a commitment to a philosophical principle. This importance accorded to the current distribution of wealth in anti-egalitarian approaches relies on a story about how that distribution emerged. If the status quo is to be defended against change on the grounds of injustice, surely it must be clear that it is not itself the product of an unjust process. We'll examine this issue in the next chapter, as well as looking at both practical and ideological objections to the consequences of equalising resources – such as the loss of liberty, infringement of property rights or detrimental effects on efficiency.

6

Property and Freedom

As long as there is any property, and while money is the standard of all other things, I cannot think that a nation can be governed either justly or happily.
Thomas Moore, 1516.[152]

In the last two chapters we've noted how the foundations of capitalist ideology include a demand for particular types of equality which have their origins in the bourgeois era – equality before the law and equality of access to political participation. We've also noted the regular failure of *really-existing capitalism* to deliver these benefits, as well as the staunch resistance to attempts to establish greater equality of resources, without which these formal, bourgeois equalities are often largely ineffective. We reviewed some eccentric (but popular) claims that gross inequality is the inevitable result of any sequence of trades or exchanges, as well as failures to account for the influence of the 'rules of the game' on these iniquitous outcomes. In this chapter, we'll look at bourgeois justifications for the *rules* of property distribution under capitalism.

In bourgeois ideology, the conceptual relationship between property and freedom is beset with contradictions. Since the seventeenth century (as we'll see later in this chapter), the *right* to hold property has been identified as an absolutely necessary component of freedom, yet the *actual ownership* of property doesn't figure at all in the criteria of freedom. According to this view, to take or infringe upon someone's property is to infringe on their freedom – yet those who hold this view manage to maintain at the very same time the belief that it's possible to be fully free while owning no property at all. The capitalist claim that a reduction in ownership of resources constitutes a reduction in the amount of freedom enjoyed by an individual is inconsistent with the fact that both the concept of capitalist society and every instance of *really-existing capitalism* include significant numbers of 'free' individuals who own no resources. (Recall from Chapter 1 that this characteristic is so central to capitalism that it is the most important factor in our definition of the capitalist economic structure.)

Another contradiction concerns the nature of voluntary actions – if a person acts voluntarily then no infringement of their freedom has occurred, but if instead that person has been forced or coerced into a course of action, then their freedom has necessarily been compromised. It's easy to see that a person handing over their wallet at gunpoint has not acted freely, but there are certainly less clear-cut cases, which require further analysis. If a person is not coerced to act in a certain way, but their options are restricted by circumstance, is their resulting action a voluntary action – can they be said to have acted freely? Capitalists argue that the proletarian, who (owning no means of production) must work or starve, nevertheless enters into a voluntary employment contract and therefore has no recourse to a complaint of exploitation. At the same time, they often complain that taxation on the profits *they could choose not to make* is a forced appropriation of their property and as such represents an infringement on their freedom.[153]

6.1 Which Property?

Before we continue, it's worth mentioning here again that there's a distinction to be drawn between *private property* and *personal property*. Although the concept of private property technically includes personal property, the term – in ideological discourse – is generally used as shorthand for 'private property in the means of production'. It is the ownership or non-ownership of factories, forests, mines, machines, land and other productive assets which we identified in Chapter 1, and which (we'll see in Chapter 9) are the source of exploitative relations in the capitalist economic structure. Most people in capitalist economies own little or no productive assets.[154] Some commentators seek to downplay this fact by arguing that many stocks and shares are owned by pension funds on behalf of a wider public, but we should be careful not to exaggerate the effects of this on ordinary people. Firstly, pension subscribers have limited effective control over the shares they 'own', but more importantly most people do not have a private pension. In the UK the median private pension contribution among the workforce and the population is zero.[155] In countries with wider private pension coverage, the amounts involved and the degree of control exercised pose no significant threat to the assertion that most people under capitalism control no means of production.

6.2 *Property and Freedom*

The prevailing ideology of the capitalist era tends to accord the institution of private property a morally privileged status whereby infringements against a person's property rights are taken to amount to infringements against that person's freedom. Attacks on property have been grouped together with attacks on the person as far back as Locke's assertion that 'no one ought to harm another in his Life, Health, Liberty or Property'[156], and capitalist theorists tend to take this assumption as read. Nozick, for example, quotes this passage and then immediately moves on to a lengthy discussion as to which types of agency might be appropriate to defend individuals against such attacks. Discussion of the validity of Locke's claim is not deemed either necessary or appropriate. Hayek is more explicit in establishing the connection between property and freedom: 'The system of private property is the most important guarantee of freedom, not only for those who own property, but scarcely less for those who do not.'[157]

It isn't only free-market fundamentalists such as Nozick and Hayek that make the connection between property and freedom. Although liberals such as Berlin – and to some extent Rawls – argue that the wealthy should be lawfully compelled through taxation or other means to make some contribution to the survival of the poor, they concede to the right-wing theorists that this constitutes a compromise between freedom and social responsibility.[158] Infringements on property are still taken to be infringements on freedom, albeit justified by the benefit in competing values. And yet a moment's consideration exposes the total absence of logic in this indispensable foundation of bourgeois thought. Whatever other virtues one might find in the system of private property it is nonsensical to argue that it increases the sum of freedom in the world. By taking private ownership of an asset a person is instantly removing the freedom of the other 7 billion or so inhabitants of the earth to use that asset as they wish. The sum of freedom in the world is immediately diminished with every transfer of a resource from non-ownership into private ownership. There may be justifications for the concept of private property, but that it increases freedom is unequivocally not one of them. Nigel Ashworth, of the right-wing lobby group IHS, spectacularly illustrates the knots people tie themselves up in when they try to argue that the institution of private property enhances freedom.[159] In his *Principles for a Free Society* (personally recommended by ERG bigwig Steve Baker and other hard-right MPs) Ashford asserts that, 'The ability to live one's own life in freedom, to pursue happiness in one's own way, requires property.'[160] Without the right to property, he continues, 'it would be impossible to live, to occupy land, to produce goods and services, to trade with others'. To the extent that Ashford's position makes any sense at all, it can only possibly be considered to relate to the *ownership* of property, not the *existence* of property. It's the actual *ownership* of land that allows one to occupy it, not the existence of the concept of ownership. People who don't own any land don't magically enjoy more freedom because of a legal framework which enables someone else to own land! In fact they are less free because the institution of private property means there are fewer places they are free to go and fewer things they are free to use. If the ability to live in freedom requires property, then Ashford should be opposed to any system under which most people don't own any property. Instead he is a fanatical supporter of a system actually defined by this feature.

The institution of private property cannot reasonably be considered to be beneficial to freedom. Private property may, of course, provide *property owners* with more freedoms than they would otherwise have, but only ever at the price of a net loss of freedom to society. If property owners would like to start justifying the system by declaring that it increases *their* freedom at the expense of everyone else's, we'll happily drop the charges of inconsistency and hypocrisy.

6.3 Property and Rights

Imagine an inventor who devises a machine which can be built easily from commonly available household objects and which is capable of treating air in such a way that those who inhale it are cured of a range of deadly diseases. Now the inventor could allow free access to his plans, or he could assert his ownership and sell the plans for £10 a time. In the first case everyone who can gain physical access to the plans and materials is free to use them. In the second case those who don't have £10 are not free to use them. There isn't a way of construing the meaning of the concept of freedom in order to find as much freedom in the world under the second scenario as under the first. The assertion of private property rights has unquestionably diminished the sum total of freedom. (Of course, in most cases, property rights have already been claimed in objects that already exist, or in the raw materials from which new objects will be made. The freedom-diminishing powers of the system of private property are not inhibited by such pre-existing ownership claims.)

The response of the bourgeois ideologue is of course to argue that the inventor would be well within their *rights* to demand a fee for access to the plans – if nothing else then just to recoup their investment in time and effort in inventing the machine in the first place. But this is an argument about rights which has no impact on the consideration of freedom. So now the conversation shifts to one about the legitimacy, or otherwise, of property rights. The first point we need to note here is that we've moved from a general theoretical claim ('if you use my property you diminish my freedom') to a specific empirical claim ('I have a right to prevent you from using this piece of my property, because I am the rightful owner.') This is important because the moral high-ground no longer lies automatically with the property owner, simply by virtue of claiming an infringement of freedom. In each individual circumstance an owner cannot resort to an over-arching theory about an abstract concept, but must come up with solid evidence of their ownership rights – the historical record is brought into play. Of course, in our daily lives, we generally accept that current legal ownership status will prevail – not least because the institutions of bourgeois society are so arranged as to make challenges impractical. But current legal status tells us that someone *does* hold ownership rights over a given resource. It is the point of a discussion such as this to ask whether that person *should* hold those ownership rights. Is the current distribution of ownership of productive resources a legitimate and just distribution?

6.4 The Distribution of Ownership

We noted in the previous chapter, on the subject of equality, that many theorists give an undue weight to the status quo. There is an assumption that in general people are entitled to what they have. But many of us wonder if this is true. Are 26 people really *entitled* to the same wealth as the poorest 3,500,000,000 people?[161] Given that millions of people die every year for want of food and millions more for want of safe drinking water, basic health care or security from violence, this is not merely an academic question. This is a matter of life and unnecessary death.[162] How do the wealthy justify their ownership, and do we accept that justification?

Probably the most influential modern attempt to justify ownership is that of Robert Nozick in his *Anarchy. State and Utopia,* the work which in 1974 'philosophically underpinned the free-market anti-welfarism of the approaching Reagan-Thatcher era'.[163] Nozick attempts to construct a theory of justice in holdings – that is, a framework whereby we can ascertain whether a particular ownership claim is just. He divides his approach into three principles, the first two of which establish the range of just means by which property may be acquired.

1. The principle of justice in acquisition refers to previously unowned property – was the property converted from an unowned status into ownership in a just manner?
2. The principle of justice in transfer refers to exchanges of property from one individual to another – was the exchange voluntary and free from fraudulent or coercive practices?

These principles extend outwards from individuals and their property to society as a whole and the distribution of resources throughout the population. If all holdings have been acquired and transferred justly, then the society-wide distribution is just. Nozick further asserts that 'whatever arises from a just situation by just steps is itself just'.[164] The idea that property must have a history of 'just transfer' is important, because without it property bought from thieves or conmen would come with legitimate property rights and such a situation would undermine the whole system. For any particular item of property, if it was acquired by its current owner through just means, from a previous owner who also acquired it by just means and so on back to the point at which it wasn't owned by anyone, and from that state it was initially acquired justly, then – and only then – can it be considered to be justly owned.

The astute reader, at this point, will be wondering where the just society Nozick describes actually exists in the real world. No one should be surprised to learn that such a society does not exist. As Nozick notes,'whether a distribution is just depends on how it came about' and it's clear that in *really-existing capitalism* much, if not most, property has an unjust transfer somewhere in its history – on anyone's criteria of justice. The details of the initial property grab are mostly lost in the mists of time – for large parts of the world we know almost nothing about the first time humans claimed permanent, bequeathable ownership over natural resources. Nozick leans heavily on Locke's ideas about original acquisition, and we'll look at some of the flaws in that approach later, but first we should note that there is **no** property under *really-existing capitalism* which meets Nozick's own criteria of justice in holdings. Recall that Nozick's criteria for an ownership claim to be considered just includes that its history of transfer from one person to another must consist only of transfers which are themselves just. Nozick also informs us in no uncertain terms that taxation is unjust. 'The minimal state is the most extensive state that can be justified,'[165] he argues, and clearly marks out all activities but protection of people and property as beyond the scope of the minimum state. Nozick insists that 'any state more extensive violates people's rights'[166] because all state activity requires taxation, and the state has no right to take people's money to pay for anything more than the very minimum necessary to protect life and property. In terms of income tax, he goes further, asserting that 'taxation of earnings from labor is on a par with forced labor'.[167]

Is there a single item of private property in the capitalist world that has a history of transfer that didn't involve taxation, or whose value has not been affected by taxation? Anything that's been transported on a publicly funded road network has – by Nozick's own standards – been tainted by unjust transfers of wealth. Anything invented or built by people who benefitted from a state-funded education derives some proportion of its value from the taxation system which Nozick declares unjust. The same goes for *any* influence of *any* publicly funded facility on the current value of *any* property. I'm fully aware that these points are to some extent technicalities. Arguing that anything that's been on a public road is not the rightful property of its owner isn't going to be well received in a casual discussion of political viewpoints. But casual discussions – when pressed – tend to fall back on deep seated assumptions that are built around the kind of ideas promoted by the likes of John Locke and Robert Nozick. We can move on to a more 'common sense' discussion of property rights in a moment, but it's important that we dismantle the philosophical scaffolding of bourgeois ideology first, so that we can see if the common sense we are then left with can carry the ideological weight demanded of it.

So far we have exposed two major pillars of the bourgeois case and we can now assert that:

1. The institution of private property does not increase the total sum of freedom in the world, and
2. Regarding taxation as theft renders all current distributions of wealth unjust.

So let's ignore for a moment Nozick's libertarian insistence that taxation is theft (or forced labour), and consider the more common sense position that taxation is a pretty reasonable approach to the funding of common goods and facilities such as roads and schools. There are arguments to be had over how much, and how to spread the burden and what to spend it on, but we can leave those for another day. Here we need to ask whether current distributions of property and resources are just, and if not then what can be done about that.

These questions lie at the heart of many day-to-day political issues. A common approach among right-wing politicians, opposing policies of wealth redistribution, is to warn that redistribution will *create* an unjust situation, whereas left-wingers argue that the current situation is already unjust and should be redressed. Denied the 'property promotes freedom' avenue, the next way in which the right seek to justify the existing distribution of wealth in any capitalist economy is to fall back on a rights-based argument – to argue (as Nozick does) that resources have accrued to those who deserve them.

A familiar incarnation of this approach is the promotion of the idea that wealth is the result of hard work. There are plenty of wealthy individuals happy to tell you that hard work is the secret to becoming rich. Multi-millionaire Tom Perkins is clear on this: 'The 1 per cent work harder.'[168] Harder than who? Coal miners? Nurses? Shopkeepers? The rest of the top 10 per cent? Tiresome Australian heiress Gina Rinehart has some similar advice for non-billionaires – simply 'become one of those people who work hard'.[169] The concept is not always expressed with quite this level of delusional vulgarity, but nevertheless it permeates capitalist society – if you work hard, you'll be rewarded. It's a persuasive message because most people in a capitalist economy live on earnings from labour – they have little wealth and what they do have, they worked for. Because most of us had to work to be able to own the things we own, it's easy to slip into the assumption that most of the things that are owned were worked for by the people who own them. Flowing naturally from this assumption that having things is the result of going to work is the impression that having more things must be the result of working harder. But we know that this is not the case. Most wealth is where it is because of ownership of productive assets, not because of hard work. In *The System – Who Rigged it, How to Fix it* Robert Reich asserts that 60 percent of household wealth in the US is in the hands of people who inherited it, not people who worked for it.[170] Although more than half of Americans own stocks, when employment-related retirement schemes are excluded a very different picture emerges – one of an America in which most people have no stake.[171] In the UK, less than 3 per cent own any stocks or shares at all and Guy Shrubsole has calculated that only 5 per cent of the land in England belongs to homeowners, with another 8.5 per cent in public ownership.172 Three decades into the twenty-first century 30 per cent of the land in England is still owned by the aristocracy and gentry! And there is little indication that this situation is likely to improve – in most OECD countries, earnings from going to work are even taxed more harshly than income from owning productive assets.[173]

Most people work hard, and their income, such as it is, is a result of that work. And clearly, many people who are very well off also work hard – but they are not well off *because* they work hard. Marx and Engels wrote of nineteenth-century capitalism that 'those who work do not gain, and those who gain do not work'.[174] While the second half of that sentiment may employ some degree of artistic licence, it's still true that hard work is not the difference between wealth and poverty. As George Monbiot has put it, 'if wealth was the inevitable result of hard work and enterprise, every woman in Africa would be a millionaire'.[175] While the wealthy may work hard, so do many who have little or nothing – the differentiating factor must be something other than hard work.

The largest single factor influencing people's wealth in modern capitalist economies is their parents' wealth[176] though other factors, such as talent, good fortune or a combination of the two obviously come into play. While it's an easily observable fact that under *really-existing capitalism* resources are not distributed according to the amount of effort expended, it's valid to ask if resources *should* be distributed on that criterion. If so, how would we measure effort? Does all work require the same effort, so that we can merely count the number of hours worked? Is physical labour harder work than mental labour? Is skilled labour harder work than unskilled – or is that the wrong way round? Should we consider the value of work to society, not just its duration or difficulty? Should there be a premium for unpleasant work? How is learning to be rewarded – or raising children, or caring for relatives?

F.A. Hayek rejects any kind of distribution of resources according to hard work, or good deeds or any other kind of 'moral merit'[177] and raises a broader objection to any 'attempts to impress upon society a deliberately chosen pattern of distribution'.[178] The pattern he then goes on to endorse is – unsurprisingly – his best attempt at formulating the already existing capitalist distribution: rewards should accrue to people according to their 'value'. How is this value to be measured? By the market of course! (Had Hayek paid more attention to Marx – or Oscar Wilde – he might have understood that there's a difference between *value* and *price*.)[179] Hayek talks about the perceived benefit to others – the value (price) of which is settled by the market and so is determined through the prism of the currently existing distribution. Hayek and his fellow free-market enthusiasts would like us to believe that the prices in a capitalist economy are somehow *natural* or *rational*. The idea is that we find the true value of something when it's offered for sale on the market. (You can insist your new product is worth ten pounds, but if no one buys it until you halve the price, then the market has 'proven' that its real value is five pounds.) The glaring hole in this argument is that the amounts people are willing or able to spend on various products is dictated by how much they have – which in turn is determined by the existing distribution of resources which is clearly not natural or rational. These theorists have invented a whole issue around this, which they call the *socialist calculation problem*. This is the claim that socialism cannot possibly work because non-market mechanisms cannot rationally calculate the values of products. The fatal flaw in the argument is that – as we've seen – capitalism doesn't rationally allocate values to products either, so we're not really losing anything. We're swapping a price-allocation system centred around the needs and wants of resource owners for a system aimed at providing for the whole community. However optimistic this sounds – however imperfect the outcome – it's important to remember that it's not the replacement for a mythical, perfectly rational system, but for one in which millions starve because available food cannot be allocated to them.

Nozick tries to tidy up Hayek's clumsy reasoning, incorporating the fact that market calculations don't reflect value or benefit per se, but 'value to those who can afford to pay' – that market value reflects a complex interaction between demand and purchasing power. Nozick rescues Hayek from his failure to notice that some people don't have much money and arrives at the less-than–elegant formula that a person will receive resources according to 'how much he benefits others who have the resources for benefitting those who benefit them'.[180] Nozick doesn't seem to mind the circularity of a distribution of resources in which value is accrued by benefitting those who already benefit from the distribution of resources. It's almost as if anything will do, if it justifies the already existing distribution.

Both Hayek and Nozick regularly ascribe a higher moral status to this approach than it deserves, by referring to the way that value accrues to 'those who benefit others', when what they mean is 'those who have something to sell which others with money are willing to pay for'. It's highly questionable – and frankly dishonest – to continually imply that, for example, a palliative care nurse 'benefits others' less than a trader at the London Metal Exchange. As Joseph Stiglitz notes, 'The model that best describes income determination at the top is not one based on individuals' contributions to society, even though of course, some at the top have made enormous contributions.'[181] Stiglitz also notes that much of the income at the top derives from 'rents' – that is taking wealth without creating it.[182] Remember that here we're discussing ownership of the means of production, not people's personal property or the goods and services they buy in order to survive and if possible to play their part in a participatory democracy. Most who work for wages are just covering their cost of living, the reproduction of themselves – of the proletariat as a class. With taxes and rent, bills, food, clothes and the cost of participating in a modern democracy, most people's income is quickly spent on outgoings and doesn't hang around long enough to become their wealth.[183] Wealth accrues largely to those who own capital, *because* they own capital, *not* because they work, although they may also work. While most work is rewarded with income – as Thomas Piketty has demonstrated – most wealth does not derive from work, however much it seems that way to those of us who only have what we've worked for.[184] The idea that the distribution of wealth or of income under capitalism reflects the amount or the value to society of the work one performs is entirely spurious.

6.5 The Origins of Property Rights

If we can see through the haze of these attempts to construct a justification of the status quo, there is actually a serious question to be discussed about just how we should approach the distribution of resources in society. Nozick rejects any attempts to allocate resources according to some kind of pattern – hard work, social good, moral merit and so on, preferring an 'entitlement' approach in which resources rightfully belong to those who are entitled to them. (His use of the term 'entitlement theory' is disingenuous as almost all approaches attempt to distribute resources according to entitlement – the disagreement is over what creates that entitlement, not whether or not something other than entitlement is the correct criteria.) What Nozick is really opposing is the idea that entitlement is based on some end-state objective or pattern of distribution, such as equality or sufficiency. He considers any assertion that all people should have an equal amount of resources – or even a sufficient amount of resources – to be a threat to the freedom of those whose resources may need to be redistributed in order to achieve such a goal. (Of course, in Nozick's world, sufficiency – the right to life – for some, should not be considered more important than any infringement on the sacred property rights of others.) We've already dispatched the idea that losing property can be treated as an infringement of freedom, by those (such as Nozick) who assert that property ownership isn't a requirement of freedom. Here we'll examine Nozick's approach from a different angle. As we've seen, he argues that people are entitled to whatever they can amass by fair means, but this approach brings a whole range of both theoretical and practical problems of its own. The practical problems begin at the beginning – with the original appropriation of the natural world into private property. At some point in pre-history, humans began to take ownership of natural resources. Instead of just using what was available, people began to claim permanent rights over things, then to extend those rights beyond their lifetimes by making their property bequeathable to their heirs. In the late seventeenth century, John Locke developed a theory of acquisition to defend the institution of private property, and to justify the increasing conversion of common land into private pasture under the process of parliamentary enclosure. (A process which by 1850 had seen the people of England deprived of their customary access to around 9 million acres of land – all in the name of freedom.)[185]

Like Nozick and Hayek's attempts to give the market a moral justification of 'benefit to others' by continually omitting the real details, Locke's justification of private property is a sleight of hand designed to attribute noble origins to theft and self-interest. Locke begins by noting that the world in its 'state of nature' existed for the benefit of all 'mankind in common' acknowledging the great difficulty in discerning 'how any one should ever come to have a *Property* in any thing'.[186] His answer to his own question attaches moral virtue to the concept of property by his assertion that it is obtained by honest toil:

> ...every man has a Property in his own Person: This no Body has any right to but himself. The Labour of his Body, and the Work of his Hands, we may say, are properly his. Whatsoever then he removes out of the State that Nature hath provided... he hath mixed his labour with...and thereby makes it his Property. It being by him removed from the common State Nature placed it in, it hath by his Labour something annexed to it, that excludes the common Right of other Men.[187]

Continuing with the veneration of Labour, Locke adds a crucial proviso, designed to ensure that the property of one person would not interfere with the freedom of others:

> For this Labour being the unquestionable Property of the Labourer, no Man but he can have a Right to what that is once joyned to, at least where there is as much and as good left for others.[188]

So property is acquired by the virtuous pursuit of labouring with ones hands, and it infringes no one's freedom because there is always 'enough and as good' left for everyone else. But clearly the amount of property in the state of nature is finite and will soon run out. Locke's proviso is inadequate in practice to perform the role he asks of it, but that's okay because he only really uses it as a means to make his formulation sound like it isn't justifying theft. Its practical value is soon superseded by a different limit on the acquisition of property – that no one may take more than they can consume before it spoils: 'Whatever is beyond this, is more than his Share, and belongs to others.'[189] So the proviso requiring each person to leave 'as much and as good' is now replaced with a requirement not to take more than one can make use of. The virtue of honest toil and the commitment to not hoard more than is useful allow Locke to maintain the impression of a moral case thus far. Next Locke extends this limit to allow individuals or families to appropriate more than they can consume, providing they barter any surplus with others so that nothing goes to waste[190] and finally, the introduction of money means that wealth can be hoarded without limit because money does not decompose, and so nothing goes to waste. The proviso which stood Locke's scheme apart from a straightforward dog-eat-dog land grab was abandoned once the 'only take what you need' limit was introduced, but that limit is first extended and then abandoned, so as to leave the proviso an empty promise for Locke and later for Nozick who takes it on board with little critical analysis.[191] (Nozick doesn't accept the proviso unquestioningly, but his discussion revolves around what is meant by 'enough and as good' and the implications of that, rather than the fact that Locke is forced to abandon the proviso because it isn't compatible with reality.) At least Murray Rothbard just admits that the proviso doesn't work and offers the alternative that, 'In fact we can generally achieve as much "access" as we want to these resources by paying the market price for them.'[192] Rothbard appears oblivious to the fact that a theory of acquisition concerns unowned property which by definition cannot be bought from the current owners. He seems to be similarly unaware that a theory of justice in acquisition by labour is supposed to allow everyone an opportunity to acquire, regardless of whether they can afford to pay the market value (which in any case doesn't exist.) That's the entire point of Locke and Nozick's attempts to inject moral virtue into the process by tying property up with phrases like 'the work of his Hands'. Though having abandoned the proviso, Locke now puts the final nail in the coffin of this idea that property ownership derives from honest toil, with his endorsement of the inheritable status of property.[193] If property is to be inherited (one of the range of transfers which Nozick lists as just) then the heirs to originally acquired land and other resources will be able to – in at least some cases – live off the ownership of those resources and not from the sweat of their brow. While Locke continues to assert that labour is *'the great Foundation of Property'*[194] throughout the *Second Treatise* his journey from proviso to limit, to extending and then abandoning that limit, combined with his endorsement of inheritance, add up to a system of property in which those who labour have none because those who don't need to labour have established a monopoly over it. (Again, remember that this is a discussion about property in the means of production, not personal belongings and notice how unrealistic is Locke's formulation that property accrues to those who mix their labour with natural resources.)

Clearly, Locke's approach to original acquisition provides little support for the idea that the current distribution of the means of production is built on just foundations. Despite the majority of transactions in recent decades being potentially just, by any reasonable measure the historical record unequivocally demonstrates that even following original acquisition an extensive period of unjust appropriation has had a profound effect on the current distribution of productive resources. The idea that 'patterned' approaches to resource distribution cannot be justified because they might upset some kind of naturally arising equilibrium is obviously unsustainable, given that we live in the real world and have got here through actual historical processes. Even Nozick accepts that this is the case, and the third of his principles of justice addresses this – albeit in a half-hearted treatment of the issue through an entirely unrealistic proposal.

Nozick's third principle concerns rectification of injustices arising from past acquisitions and transfers. He suggests that some kind of one-off payment could be made to victims of injustice. No details are provided but there is the impression of some kind of once-and-for-all redistribution to rectify all past injustices, after which careful adherence to the principle of justice in transfer will ensure a just distribution in future.[195] As a thought experiment this might have potential, but as a practical suggestion for a policy approach, it's pure fantasy. The historical record is both clear enough to prove beyond doubt that (at least) large chunks of property have ended up where they are through unjust transactions, it's also murky enough to prevent any grand-rectification of the kind envisaged by Nozick. There was an attempt, during the aftermath of the French Revolution, to conduct something like the grand redistribution which Nozick imagines is feasible. It was less ambitious than Nozick's position requires but it still proved untenable. The idea was to abolish the privileges of the nobility, but to retain property ownership which derived from contractual exchange. Such a process would require some means of distinguishing between a privilege and a contractually justified right in each instance of ownership. This was clearly a move in the direction of what we've termed bourgeois equality, as it sought to abolish ownership claims which stemmed from expressions of social status.[196] Piketty suggests that the exercise alerted the revolutionary legislators to the perils of such a process: 'Provided one went far enough, perhaps centuries back in time, it was obvious to everyone that violence played a part in the acquisition of most seigniorial rights, which stemmed from conquest and serfdom. If one followed this logic to the end it was clear that the very idea of a contractual origin to property rights was pure fiction'.[197]

So we have a principle in which labour is exalted and held to be the virtue by which property ownership has been distributed, being used to justify a system that embodies the exact opposite, and which rewards the non-labouring, property-owning bourgeoisie at the expense of the dispossessed, labouring proletariat. Locke's insistence that labour *'puts the greatest part of Value upon Land,* without which it would scarcely be worth any thing'[198] is quickly forgotten after a generation or two of inheritance. The land which supposedly is almost worthless without labour becomes the fanatically guarded property of the bourgeois, while labour – for Locke, the source of value – is the poorly rewarded realm of the proletarian. Three-and-a-half centuries later Thomas Piketty provides a wealth of data to prove that inequality of capital is greater than inequality of income, at all times and in all places – largely because wealth accrues to those who own wealth, not to those who work.[199] Again, we find *really-existing capitalism* failing to live up to its ideological foundations. As Robert Reich notes, 'dynastic wealth runs counter to the ideal of...meritocracy...it puts economic power into the hands of a relatively small number of people who have never worked...It creates a self-perpetuating aristocracy that is antithetical to democracy.'[200]

6.6 Property and Productivity

Having failed to provide a theoretical justification for the concept of property or an empirical justification for its current distribution, bourgeois ideologues have one more trick up their sleeve – again dating back to Locke's *Second Treatise on Government* and developed by Nozick in *Anarchy, State and Utopia*. According to Locke, God gave the land 'to the industrious and rational'[201] so that 'he who appropriates Land to himself by his Labour, does not lessen but increases the common stock of Mankind'.[202] (The position here is that while they may have taken all the resources, they are so industrious and they produce so much that everyone else is better off for it. It's the origin of the proposal that even though your share of the pie may be small, capitalism makes the whole pie bigger, so you should be grateful.)[203] Nozick picks up this theme and modifies Locke's *proviso* so that the limit of the property a person may claim for themselves is not that it must leave sufficient for others, but that it must not leave others *worse off*. But 'worse off', for Nozick, does not mean 'unable to use the thing which they are now not free to use' – even though, by Nozick's own criteria, in which property and freedom trump all other benefits, this undoubtedly *does* leave people worse off. Nozick here decides that being 'worse off' equates to suffering a *net loss*, and that the person best placed to weigh up gains and losses and to decide which way the scales have tipped is Robert Nozick. He envisages some kind of compensation which would be due to those deprived of the chance to own property but he dismisses suggestions that such compensation might consist of sufficiency – 'a socially guaranteed minimum provision' – as too generous.[204] The compensation which Nozick has in mind for those rendered propertyless by the march of capitalism is that they are able to live in a capitalist world. Because capitalism is more efficient and productive than pre-capitalist systems, the dispossessed proletarians will be rewarded with the abundance of capitalist production. Well, a small part of it. Three-and-a-half billion of them can share the same amount as 26 property-owning bourgeois billionaires, and they can work for it instead of relaxing on a yacht while watching it pour in. Although Nozick's approach to this issue is particularly crass, he's not alone in imagining that it's possible for those who have appropriated the planet to compensate the rest of us for our loss. Whereas Nozick thinks that the wonders of capitalism should be compensation enough, others are more generous. Thomas Paine, for example, proposed a one-off payment and a pension 'as a compensation in part, for the loss of his or her natural inheritance, by the introduction of the system of landed property'.[205] While Paine betrays his understanding that the system of property itself has robbed most people of something which is rightfully theirs, and therefore should know that a cash payment offers no kind of compensation, Nozick is more internally consistent in that he appears to really believe his own publicity and that property owners really are *entitled* to their holdings.

Bourgeois philosophers assign a morally privileged status to the concept of private property in order to characterise attempts to redistribute resources as attacks on their freedom. And yet they argue that those permanently excluded from property ownership still enjoy full freedom. Although these theorists venerate property to such an extent that to infringe on theirs is an attack on their freedom – even to the point that they often regard taxation as theft – they are also able to consider that denying others the opportunity to own property is not an infringement on *their* freedom, providing they're permitted to toil in return for an income, which may or may not be sufficient for their survival. And that if it isn't sufficient for their survival, then their death should not be considered an infringement on their freedom. And they hold all of these opinions at the same time, and with a straight face.

Earlier in this chapter we summarised our findings to that point as having exposed two major pillars of the bourgeois case and we asserted that:

1. The institution of private property does not increase the total sum of freedom in the world, and
2. Regarding taxation as theft renders all current distributions of wealth unjust – and is inconsistent with regarding wage labour as a voluntary contract.

We can now add:

3. Wealth under capitalism is not distributed according to work, effort, value to society or any other index of 'moral merit',
4. The historical record provides no justification for the current distribution of resources in capitalist societies, and
5. The productive advantages of capitalism do not provide sufficient justification for inequalities of resource distribution since, even by the measure preferred by bourgeois ideologues, *income* cannot compensate for exclusion from *ownership*. (This is particularly true when the income also has to be earned as wages, which makes it remuneration for labour, not compensation for having no property.)

So having expressed significant dissatisfaction with the capitalist approach to the relationship between freedom and property, it would be useful here to look at some ideological principles which might provide a framework for potential alternatives.

Firstly, we should establish that freedom is an objective state – the presence or absence of which is not determined by people's claims to hold certain rights – whether those rights are considered to be natural, human, civil or legal. This approach is in contrast to the broad consensus of opinion among capitalist philosophers that freedom is contingent upon rights.

If, for example, you decide to pitch a tent on my property, that's viewed as an infringement on my freedom to use my property as I see fit – because I have a *right* to refuse you access to my property. If I prevent you from pitching your tent on my land, however, that's not viewed as an infringement on your freedom to pitch your tent wherever you wish, because you have no *right* to pitch your tent on my land. While this might seem like a technicality it's important because the concept of freedom comes with a built-in implication of moral virtue. If we allow the term 'freedom' to be used out of place, we risk attributing moral value to morally neutral situations. The idea that your freedom is not curtailed *if I am within my rights* to prevent you from camping in my field might sound reasonable, but it goes against what we normally think of when we talk about freedom. This idea that a person's freedom is not diminished if they have no right to do the thing they are being prevented from doing entails the idea that a prisoner's freedom is not diminished providing they have been properly convicted – if society is within its rights to lock them in a cell. This is clearly at odds with any normal understanding of the concept of freedom or use of the term in general conversation. No one thinks a prisoner is 'free' just because they have been properly convicted. And yet it's this interpretation of the meaning of freedom which props up so much of the moral case for capitalism. Under the bourgeois conception of freedom, only unlawful, or unethical, or otherwise *unjust* acts can restrict a person's freedom. Legal acts, such as property ownership, are not deemed to be restrictions on the freedoms of non-owners. In general, according to this view, we enjoy the freedom to do things we cannot do, providing the reason why we cannot do them is deemed a just restriction.

A cynical observer might suggest that a capitalist conception of freedom has to work in this way because it's the only way to justify people dying for want of resources while others possess more resources than they could ever make any use of. While *life* and *liberty* enjoy equal billing it's no one's moral responsibility to give up their liberty to save the lives of others. And while liberty is tied to property then addressing global hunger remains in the *nice idea* folder, not the *moral duty* inbox. As we've seen, the bourgeois conception of what is just has no basis in theoretical consistency or historical fact, so the arbiter of justice tends to default to property rights established by legal frameworks, which are devoid of historical justification and which the capitalists themselves reject when it comes to regarding taxation as an infringement upon freedom. And around in circles we go following bourgeois attempts to dress up self-interest as logic or ethics or rights or historical precedent or anything but what it actually is. As J.K. Galbraith noted in 1964, 'The modern conservative is engaged in one of man's... oldest exercises in moral philosophy. That is the search for a superior moral justification for selfishness.'[206]

6.7 The Possible and the Permissible

Jonathan Wolff suggests a taxonomy of types of access to freedoms which may help us to see the differences in approach to this issue. He draws the distinction between *possibility* and *permissibility*: capitalist ideology asserts that freedom to do something is achieved if there is no rule forbidding it – if the act is *permissible*. Socialist ideology demands that an act is *possible* before recognising a person's freedom to perform it. Wolff suggests that the left tend to place too much emphasis on the possibility, which the right ignore in their focus on the permissibility.[207] How can the importance of possibility be overstated though? If we accept that the meaning of freedom entails that having the freedom to do something requires that we are able to do that thing, then freedom *requires* possibility. That an action is permissible is not a sufficient condition of it being possible, or of anyone being free to do it. It is *possibility* alone which gives freedom its meaning – the idea that permissibility confers freedom is nothing but a bourgeois illusion.

The root of the permissible/possible debate lies in one of the central distinctions between socialism and capitalism. Capitalist ideology, as we have seen in chapters 4 and 5, recognises that there is an innate equality in our shared membership of humankind, that there is *something* of which we are entitled to equal amounts, just by virtue of our being human. But capitalism demands that we draw the line at equality before the law and equality of political participation – that these bourgeois equalities are all that freedom requires. From this perspective, outside of causing harm to others anything may be *permissible.* If some things for some people are not *possible,* then that's just the way of the world and can't be helped – even if the things that aren't possible include having enough food to stay alive or having access to safe drinking water. Capitalists might find it unfortunate that some people starve to death because others have established a monopoly of resources, but in their schema, the freedom of those who die isn't infringed by those who take all the resources. In bourgeois ideology, freedom to be alive doesn't trump freedom to own property and here again we find the 'logic' of capitalism disappearing up its own inconsistency because we started this summary of the bourgeois position with the qualification that '*Outside of causing harm to others,* anything is permissible.' But owning all the resources and denying others the means of survival does – on any reasonable understanding – cause harm to those denied the necessities of life. Socialists place your freedom not to starve above my freedom to mark out a chunk of the natural world as mine and mine alone. The only way to deliver real freedom to real people in their real lives is to back up the formal benefit of **permissibility** with the material benefit of **possibility**. *Really-existing freedoms* will always require access to resources, and the redistribution of resources to achieve that end is not in itself an infringement on anyone's freedom. The right to survival should always take precedence over the right to own private property. As Gerrard Winstanley argued while John Locke was still in short trousers, 'A man had better to have had no body than to have no food for it.'[208]

6.8 Distributive Justice

If then, we are to make some provision for a different distribution of resources to that which emerges via the market from the dark recesses of pre-history, what principles should guide that redistribution? An obvious candidate for socialists is Marx's formulation in his *Critique of the Gotha Programme* that resources should be allocated 'from each according to his ability, to each according to his need'.[209] Unfortunately this doesn't give us much in the way of actual policies to go on, but even leaving aside any practical limitations, Nozick raises an objection to the principle of Marx's dictum. Nozick argues that 'from each' and 'to each' should not be treated as independent questions. Products, he reminds us, don't just pop into existence devoid of human activity, they are brought into existence *by* someone and that someone already has a claim on them, before any redistributive considerations about who might 'need' them come into play.[210] Obviously Nozick's veneration of the noble labourer doesn't stretch here to viewing the goods as belonging to the person whose *labour* created them – rather it's the owners of the means of production whose interests must be defended. We might ask, though, why Nozick starts his analysis with products and their producers, rather than with people and their needs. People are born with needs and they continue to have needs throughout life – for nutrition, shelter, healthcare, education and so on. But people are not always productive, even in the widest possible sense. Some people will always be unable to work. In a civilised society children and the elderly are not expected to work and we would all be better off if a greater range of human activities were excluded from the influence of the market. (What benefit is to be gleaned from applying the profit motive to palliative care or mental health provision, for example?) We might ask why Nozick would begin his enquiry into distribution with the production process, not the people – with the products, not the needs. The products only exist because of the needs, so it seems reasonable to ask at the outset which needs – whose needs – will the products be meeting? In truth – and despite Nozick's objections – that is how the market works under capitalism.

Products are created to meet a demand, the only difference is that in a capitalist economy 'demand' is related to need through the vector of *ability to pay*. Although this system has – for a few hundred years – enabled huge technological advances which have created the productive capacity to provide civilised living conditions for all, it is a system which is incapable of delivering that change. It's time now to consider systems designed to meet the needs of humanity *as they are*, not as they appear through the distorted lens of the market.

Largely, Nozick's objection centres around his view that distribution must be based on historical factors not 'end-state' considerations. He argues that any system in which distribution is organised under a 'patterned' principle – such as equality or sufficiency – only takes account of what people have, not how or why they came to have what they have. As such these systems miss out a crucial aspect of justice in distribution. Did someone *deserve* to have more or less than others? He rightly points out that if we look at who is or isn't in prison at any given time, we don't say that *A* has been treated unfairly compared to *B* just because *A* is in prison and *B* is not. We need to know what they each have done before we can decide on the justice or otherwise of their respective predicaments. We need to know their stories.[211] Nozick argues that the same is true of wealth distributions. We need to see the historical record, to know whether *A* and *B* acquired their wealth justly or otherwise, before we can know if they deserve their respective fortunes. As we've seen, though, while Nozick's criticisms of 'patterned' distributions make some telling points, his preferred 'entitlement' distribution – based supposedly on the historical record – is even more vulnerable to criticism. The paucity of historical evidence, the certainty of unjust transfer in the parts of the record which do exist, the circular logic in considering taxation as both theft and legitimate transaction in the same breath and the reliance on the total fantasy of some *grand redistribution* all deliver fatal blows to Nozick's preferred approach.

There is no reason, though, why an approach to justice in the distribution of the means of production has to fit into one or other of Nozick's categories. The distinction isn't hard and fast anyway – as is evidenced by Nozick's confusion regarding Hayek's market-driven 'pattern'. Nozick classifies Hayek's distribution according to 'perceived benefits to others' as a 'patterned' or 'end-state' system, despite its clear reliance on the historical record of what *A* has done to benefit *B*. Similarly, distributions based on 'reward for effort' or some other form of moral merit clearly rely on some knowledge of how people have behaved in order to work out their just allocation of resources. Although Nozick's criticisms of the ethical basis of 'patterned' or 'end-state' approaches to the distribution of resources don't stand up to rigorous examination, his exposure of the practical limitations of such ideas does show them to be incompatible with a system of private ownership. Nozick proposes a thought experiment to illustrate that any 'patterned' distribution is vulnerable to becoming 'unpatterned' – to losing the distribution its creators deemed desirable – through innocent transactions.[212] He invites the reader to imagine that a grand redistribution of resources has taken place and that everything is distributed in accordance with their preferred pattern – equality perhaps. From that point he describes how someone – basketball star Wilt Chamberlain in Nozick's example – becomes fantastically rich through a series of voluntary exchanges which no reasonable person could consider unjust or exploitative. In the example, a million people pay to see Chamberlain play over the course of a season and he receives 25¢ from each ticket, leading to his accumulation of $250,000. (Remember that Nozick was writing in 1974.) Thus the preferred egalitarian distribution of resources is destroyed by a series of innocent, non-exploitative transactions. The advocates of egalitarian distribution, he argues, must devise policies which intervene in this series of free, voluntary transactions to confiscate most of Chamberlain's justly acquired wealth in order to restore their preferred distribution. Nozick's 'Wilt Chamberlain problem' is only half the story, though. The situation is compounded by the introduction of what we might call the *Lintilla Problem* (after Douglas Adams' infinitely replicating clones).[213] In this analogy, the Lintillas represent human generations – a population which is never static, meaning that we can't ever distribute resources once-and-for-all because by the time we had even conceived of such a distribution thousands of births and deaths would have rendered it obsolete. Free-market mechanisms are not sophisticated enough to continually redistribute resources in a way that maintains distributive justice in the face of new people being born every day. Distributive justice cannot be achieved or maintained through a mechanism of private property. The ownership benefits of wealth-creating property – of the means of production – must be aggregated in some way.

Between them, Wilt Chamberlain and Lintilla make the idea of an egalitarian distribution of property ownership appear as a practical impossibility. And to some extent it is – but that doesn't necessarily rule out the possibility of an egalitarian society – or at least a more egalitarian society than is currently the case. Nozick habitually ignores any distinction between property ownership in general and ownership of the means of production. He also conveniently picks an extremely atypical example of how a very wealthy person becomes wealthy. As we've seen, he acknowledges the *dirty history* responsible for a large proportion of the current distribution of wealth, but offers little more than a shrug and a childlike fantasy as a solution. In all of these matters we are entitled to expect more from Nozick, but for perhaps the most important failing of his viewpoint he could be forgiven. The distinction between wealth and income was obviously a known issue when Nozick was writing, but the significance of its impact on patterns of inequality has grown in recent years with the availability of more data and the work of economists such as Thomas Piketty, Robert Reich and Joseph Stiglitz, as we've noted in earlier chapters.

Perhaps a part of the solution to the failings of both the historical record approach of Nozick and the 'patterned' approach of egalitarian theorists is to develop different strategies for wealth and for income. Distinctions already exist in tax regimes and other financial instruments, but a different conception of the rules of ownership provides a new set of options. As we've seen, the inequalities of capitalism are often excused on the grounds that a smaller share of pie is compensated for by the efficiency of capitalism managing to increase the overall size of the pie. But maybe we should admit that there are two pies. The income pie is supposedly distributed in accordance with effort, but the share of those who work keeps getting smaller. Meanwhile, the wealth pie gets ever bigger but most people don't own even a crumb of that pie.

Rules regarding ownership of wealth, we might decide, could be further divided into those which apply to personal possessions and those which apply to the means of production. Only a few hundred years ago a large proportion of the means of production in England were owned in common, with different individuals enjoying different rights of use and gaining different benefits. We certainly don't want to revert to a feudal ownership model, but we should be aware that a change in our understanding of the way ownership works is not such a big deal. We've weathered these changes before, and in the name of progress we need to weather them again. Given the problematic nature of existing distributions of the means of production which we've discussed in this chapter, and the practical impossibility of maintaining an egalitarian distribution of individual ownership, it's worth looking again at the possibility of shared ownership of productive resources.

For some, alarm bells will be ringing just now – or hammers

and sickles will be clanging – but our discussion in the first two chapters of this work should have dispelled any concerns on that front. To recap – experiments with regimes favouring communal ownership in the twentieth century predictably failed, due to the backward nature of the economic and political landscapes in which they took place. Without the abundance delivered by the technological advances of the capitalist epoch, and without the institutions and political culture of mature democracies, attempts to move to a system of public ownership are, and always have been, unlikely to succeed. As we progress through the twenty-first century and into the age of AI, we might very well find that experiments with collective ownership are the most likely to deliver the solutions to the problems we now face. As we've seen, many on the right will resist any threat to the system of private property, but their justification wholly depends upon one fairytale or another about past justice and how we arrived at the current distribution. It's time to reject this preposterous con trick and to recognise that the system of private property inhibits freedom, and that its current distribution is an affront to logic and history, as well as to the concept of justice.

In this chapter we've addressed concerns about the moral justification of attempts to redress the iniquities of current resource distributions, and found the objections to a more equitable distribution to be little more than self-interest dressed up as moral imperatives. Yet those who benefit from the iniquities of the current distribution might find themselves unconvinced by our arguments, and *some* of them will resist change just as fiercely as if they were right. So having concluded the ideological argument, we now need to address the practical question of how we might move to a more equitable distribution in the face of resistance from those whose self-interest is well-served by capitalism. We rejected the viability of a sudden and forcible uprising in Chapter 2, so we'll need to explore ideas about the kind of mechanism by which resources might be successfully transferred out of private hands into public ownership. We'll address exactly that question in Chapter 9, but first we'll look at how we might have to change our approach to the concepts of work and money in the transition away from a capitalist economic structure.

Part III
Progress

7

Work

There seems a general rule that, the more obviously one's work benefits other people, the less one is likely to be paid for it
David Graeber, 2013[214]

7.1 Work and Virtue

We noted in Chapter 6 the importance attributed to labour in Locke's account of the origins of private property. For Locke, property ownership is given a morally privileged position through an association with honest toil:

> ...every man has a *Property* in his own *Person*: This no Body has any right to but himself. The *Labour* of his Body, and the *Work* of his Hands, we may say, are properly his. Whatsoever then he removes out of the State that Nature hath provided... he hath mixed his *Labour* with...and thereby makes it his *Property*. It being by him removed from the common State Nature placed it in, it hath by his *Labour* something annexed to it, that excludes the common Right of other Men.[215]

Of course, even a conceptual connection between actual work and ownership of land was fairly spurious in Locke's account of the history of property acquisition, and disappears entirely within a few generations of property inheritance, but the idea of the moral virtue of labour remained prevalent. By the nineteenth century, despite being entirely obvious to anyone that the *distribution* of wealth and income were entirely unrelated to the distribution of effort or toil, the idea that all (or most) value is *created* by labour was widespread. The *Labour Theory of Value* is often associated with Marx, but was common currency among classical economists before Marx's time. This veneration of labour was not restricted to economists – in his first annual message to congress Abraham Lincoln reflected the mood of the times: 'Labor is prior to and independent of capital. Capital is only the fruit of labor and could not have existed if labor had not first existed. Labor is the superior of capital and deserves much the higher consideration.'[216] It's nice that toil is held in such high regard among the bourgeois establishment, those who – as Russell notes – 'preach the dignity of labour, while taking care themselves to remain undignified in this respect'.[217] But such regard rarely extends to rewarding effort at anything above the lowest possible rate. In fact, the mantra of capitalists everywhere is that their first duty is to shareholders. It would be a dereliction of this duty to purchase labour power (and associated skills and experience) at anything but the lowest price available. The price of labour under capitalism – like the price of any commodity – is determined through the mechanism of the 'free' market, which is very good at rewarding innovation in profitable fields, but outstandingly poor at rewarding hard work.

David Graeber notes that there is a theological aspect to 'the old idea that work forms character', which dates back to the pre-industrial past. Although the apprenticeship system in medieval England clearly performed functional, practical roles in terms of training, education and social cohesion, Graeber suggests that there was also a strong moral component to the practice, and to the concept of work itself, which he argues was viewed as an act of moral rectitude – like a 'secular hair shirt'.[218] The concept and practice of work, though, was significantly altered by the industrial revolution. In pre-industrial settings, working hours were determined by the rhythms of the seasons, both in terms of available daylight and the types and amounts of work to be done. Even many non-agricultural occupations in pre-industrial economies were influenced by the seasons – in determining availability of materials and demand for products and services. It was the factory system which was really responsible for the widespread adoption of standardised, regular working hours and it is this difference which has skewed our moral judgement in relation to work and employment. Although the employment contract and the 'voluntary exchange' of labour power for wages create an impression of a strictly functional business transaction, there is – and *should be* – a moral dimension to the organisation of work in society. There is work to be done, to provide the means of life and civilisation, and there are people who cannot work (children, the elderly, the disabled and unwell) which means that those who are able to, have an obligation to work, and to do so to a greater extent than to provide for themselves.[219] We *should* feel a moral obligation to contribute to society and to civilisation. But that's an entirely different proposition to feeling a moral obligation to work 40 hours a week in a call centre, reading scripts to dissatisfied customers. We've taken our eye off the ball here and conflated being useful with being in employment. Work may be its own reward, but pointless drudgery is not. If contributing to the promotion of a civilised society is important to people's sense of fulfilment at work, a set of objectives focused on meeting society's needs provides a far more satisfactory solution than the labour market under capitalism in the twenty-first century.

7.2 Beyond the Labour Market

In Chapter 3 we looked at the coming changes to the employment landscape in the face of further automation and the continued development of artificial intelligence. If we're going to meet these challenges positively, take them as an opportunity to move forward and avoid the usual divisive chaos that comes from automation under capitalism then we need to develop a new approach to the relationship between effort and reward. Perhaps instead of effort and reward we need to think more in terms of rights and responsibilities. People have natural *rights* – or human rights if you prefer – including the right to a dignified life on a planet that can easily afford such luxuries.[220] On the other hand, even in the most automated future imaginable, there is still quite a lot of work that will need to be done – and we share a collective *responsibility* to ensure that the work gets done so that those rights are maintained for everyone.

It's clear that we cannot rely on market mechanisms to assign value to different types of work, to ensure that the work that gets done is the work we need to be done, to regulate supply and demand of skills and training for employment, to set rewards and incentives for different career paths or to inspire the type of innovations most required by society, or by civilisation. Outside of the philosophical commitment to the bourgeois conceptions of freedom and property which we examined and found wanting in Chapter 6, there is absolutely no reason to think that all of these requirements must be met by a single mechanism – the labour market is not the sole and final arbiter of which work is to be done, who is to do it and how much they'll be paid.

Once we stop treating the market as some kind of divine measure of value, we become free to look at a range of options and to consider separately each of the roles currently left to the labour market. We can start this process by looking at:

1. The distribution of effort, which can be further divided into:
   –the distribution of tasks – *what needs to be done*, and
   –the distribution of people – *who will do it*

2. The distribution of rewards, including:
   –rewards for effort, skills and unpleasant work, and
   –rewards for innovation

7.3 The Distribution of Effort

If we're to consider alternatives to using the market as the determining factor in the distribution of effort in society, we need to look at two central issues – what needs to be done and who needs to do it.

In terms of determining what needs to be done – where we need to direct our efforts – we need to consider which currently existing tasks will be automated out of existence, but also which will become redundant as we move away from a market-centred model for organising productive activity. The business of affiliate marketing, as we noted in Chapter 3, is one example of a collection of tasks which have no role to play outside of a market-driven economy. Advertising and marketing in general will likely play a much-reduced role, and focus more on providing information than telling people that their life has no meaning if their phone is more than 6 months old.

From an anthropological perspective, Graeber argues that many occupations in modern capitalist economies are of no discernible use to anyone. He refers to these as *Bullshit Jobs* – which he defines as 'a form of paid employment that is so completely pointless, unnecessary or pernicious that even the employee cannot justify its existence even though, as part of the conditions of employment, the employee feels obliged to pretend that this is not the case'.[221] Graeber cites a YouGov poll of UK workers which found that only 50 per cent of those who had full-time jobs were entirely sure their job made any sort of meaningful contribution to the world, and 37 per cent were quite sure it did not.[222] Even allowing for an element of employees alienated from the rationale of their role in the production process, or unable to identify the value of the process to which their work contributes, these figures are startling – over a third of employees can't all be entirely mistaken about whether their role makes any meaningful contribution to the world. This figure necessarily rules out people involved in the production of obviously useful items – food, medicines or hospital equipment, cars and trains, houses, washing machines and dartboards, for example. Similarly, those working in health, social care, education, transport or construction are likely to be able to discern value to society in their work. So these high percentages of bullshit jobs are necessarily concentrated in limited sectors of industry and crop up largely in office work, centred around the production of information. In my personal experience in this kind of role, the people for whom the information is collected usually lack the skills, time or inclination to gain any meaningful value from the data anyway. In other scenarios the information might prove useful in an immediate sense, but to serve an ultimately meaningless end.

Somewhere between a half and a third of our workforce are occupied in pointless activity and at the same time we are chronically short of nurses, doctors, social workers, youth support workers and teachers. We don't have enough people in support roles for all of those occupations, or maintaining infrastructure or building houses. More than 3 years after the deaths of 72 people in the Grenfell Tower fire and over a year since the inquiry recommended that similar buildings receive treatment to prevent further tragedies, work is still yet to begin.[223] Our approach needs to find a better mechanism for identifying the goals that would benefit society and distributing our collective efforts to achieve those goals.

The second element of the process of distributing effort relates to the allocation of effort between people. As we noted in Chapter 3, the standard response of capitalist economies to waves of automation is to continue to overwork an ever-decreasing number of people, while disowning any responsibility to the rest. In *Rise of the Robots – Technology and the Threat of a Jobless Future,* Martin Ford predicts that twenty-first century automation will fail to generate new forms of employment and that expanding education and training will not help as there will simply be very little demand for labour, however skilled. Ford envisages a future of 'techno feudalism' in which the well-off live in gated communities and the rest of us become superfluous.[224] Jerry Kaplan proposes in *Humans Need Not Apply: A Guide to Wealth and Work in the Age of Artificial Intelligence* that every 10-year-old in the US should be assigned a kind of federal earnings/benefit account, with those who grow up to find employment subsidising the rest, who would occupy themselves with volunteer work.[225] In *The Second Machine Age*, Brynjolfsson and McAfee suggest a negative income tax to support the newly unemployed masses.[226] The problem with all of these approaches, though, is that they all assume that we must inevitably meet technological advances by throwing some people out of work and on to the scrapheap while others remain over-employed with 'most of life and time and energy spent joylessly producing means to imperative ends'[227]. Once we remember that the point of productive activity is to meet the needs of the population and that the way to decide who does what in the workforce doesn't have to involve the market, it becomes astoundingly obvious that there's no need to expect an ever-dwindling number of workers to do all the work, while an ever-growing army of unemployed look on in poverty.

Given that automation and the advance of AI are going to be having a dramatic effect on the employment landscape, there will be considerably less to do in some areas. Our neglected infrastructure, ageing populations and history of underfunding all kinds of services centred around improving the quality of life mean that there's quite a lot more to do in other areas. Obviously, people can't suddenly move from what Graeber refers to as a 'bullshit job' herding spreadsheets around an office network and then retrain immediately to become an effective ICU nurse or railway maintenance engineer. But overtime, we need a long-term plan to redirect our efforts into work that we all know needs doing – work which is far more important than yet another PowerPoint slide on the Acme Corporation's EBITDA figure for Q3. If we stop treating the labour market as the sole arbiter of what gets done, and who by, then the advance of automation and AI can – at last – fulfil its promise of reducing the total amount of work that needs to be done.

An obvious objection to this approach will come from those asking how we would pay for all of these workers spending their time meeting our needs instead of keeping Jeff Bezos in yachts. Those concerns are addressed in Chapter 8. In Chapter 9 we'll look at some practical policies regarding the relationship between work, reward and income, but first we'll address a different aspect of the work-reward relationship – the concern that any non-market approach will break the system of incentive and reward, without which nothing will get done.

7.4 The Distribution of Reward

In 1987, as the Soviet Union was sleepwalking to its demise, Sergey Vikulov (the poet, not the ice hockey player) wrote in *Pravda* on the problem of motivating the peasants in a command economy: 'In the old days they did not work because they knew they would get nothing. Now they do not work because they know they will be paid anyway.'[228] The question of motivation had been an issue in the USSR and is one which market-enthusiasts regularly level at any proposals for distributing effort and reward in any post-market economy. In an ideal-typical free market the motivation for the propertyless to work is clear – the alternative is starvation. Many industrial democracies have mitigated the excesses of the free market and upgraded the non-working 'option' from starvation to destitution, or in particularly generous cases to mere poverty. A defining characteristic of the socialist economic structure is that people are not forced to choose between exploitative employment and poverty or destitution. For many, some kind of universal income scheme is an attractive way of alleviating the work-or-starve mentality of capitalism. In Chapter 9 I'll explain why I don't favour UBI as a solution – though it may be suitable as a temporary measure in emergencies such as the Covid-19 pandemic. The worry – for many working people in capitalist economies – is that if we guarantee a decent and dignified standard of living, regardless of whether people work or not, then some will take advantage and spend their days fishing or bonding with their children, or learning origami, rather than working, and that will mean more toil and less reward for the rest of us. But removing the market mechanism doesn't have to mean free money for everyone, or that there won't be a requirement for those who are able to make a contribution to society to do so. (Though, as we'll see, undercutting our reliance on the labour market will help us to make the most of technological advances and to share the benefits of such progress much more equally than has been the case in the past – and the upshot of that might well be more fishing, more bonding and more elegant paper swans...)

Although we've noted that the labour market is particularly poor in rewarding workers proportionately to their efforts or usefulness or any other just or logical measure, it does provide a means of allocating rewards for different types of employment – and indeed, allocating people to different roles. There's no reason to imagine – although many choose to do so – that a post-capitalist employment landscape would provide exactly equal rewards for all workers. Removing the market or partially replacing it perhaps with a system in which a basic wage is supplemented with additional rewards for certain features of employment (particularly hard or unpleasant or socially valuable or skilled work, for example) would provide the opportunity to dispense with some of the more extreme and unjustified differentials in earned income. So the motivation to work would remain just as strong under this kind of system as it currently is under the free labour market, the difference is that higher wages would reward work on the basis of its social utility, rather than on its capacity to furnish a profit for shareholders.

We'll also need to reward innovation but we should note that the kind of innovation which is handsomely rewarded by the free market is not necessarily innovation that has anything to offer humanity. Throughout the industrial revolution and into the late twentieth century there may have been a convenient overlap between innovations which increased wealth and innovations which drove productive capacity forward, but this relationship is – or was – specific to a given range of technological development. We've moved on and outgrown the happy accident of that overlap. Many of the best rewarded innovators under our present system are not the people who solve problems or cure diseases, but those who work out how to monetise such advances. So as well as needing to rethink our approach to rewarding work, perhaps we'll need some new ideas about rewarding innovation too, though it shouldn't take much to improve on the current system, under which rewards for innovation are haphazard and unpredictable. Financially speaking, Crick and Watson were considerably less well rewarded for their pioneering discovery of the structure of DNA, than was Professor Rubik for his cube.

8

Money

This planet...had a problem – which was this: most of the people living on it were unhappy for most of the time. Many solutions were suggested for this problem, but most of these were largely concerned with the movements of small green pieces of paper, which is odd because on the whole it wasn't the small green pieces of paper that were unhappy
Douglas Adams, 1978[229]

Hopefully, by this point, it's clear that replacing the capitalist economic structure isn't going to happen overnight. There are two implications of this. Firstly, that it would be fruitless for me to speculate about the precise details of the post-capitalist world. In the same way that the exact workings of capitalism were not available to the imagination of John Locke or the architects of the Glorious Revolution, neither is a blueprint for whatever comes next available to us today. Secondly, though, if it's going to be a long time coming, it makes sense to get on with it – particularly given that capitalism is entirely incapable of addressing the climate emergency we now face – so now is the time to start to look into changes that can move us in the right direction. In an unusually lucid moment in 1982, Milton Friedman noted that in times of crisis 'the actions that are taken depend on the ideas that are lying around'.[230] So now it's time to get some ideas on the table, some suggestions for deliberation – so that they're out there and being discussed and argued over when the time comes. This final section aims to contribute to that process, both in terms of suggesting some original ideas and of rounding up some of the best ideas already out there. As Thomas Piketty notes in *Capital and Ideology*, our purpose for now should be 'to begin the debate, not to end it'.[231]

While any policy which improves the lives of ordinary people is a step in the right direction, we must be careful to distinguish between those which are merely mitigating the ills of capitalism and those which genuinely move us closer to a post-capitalist system. The former can only be temporary measures while we aim for the latter. In many cases, the ideas we put forward today might turn out to be stepping stones towards bigger and better ideas in the future. In some cases, these ideas – or some variant of them – have been tried or are currently in operation somewhere in the world. In other cases, they are still at the drawing board stage and will need further work before they can be incorporated into a coherent economic, social and political programme. As we noted in Chapter 1, the revolutionary transition from one economic structure to another requires numerous experiments and will inevitably include some wrong turns and false starts. This chapter begins with a look at some approaches which can help to break down embedded attitudes to the current distribution of wealth, to the way we understand the workings of the capitalist economy and to the bourgeois conception of what wealth and property mean.

First up is Modern Monetary Theory, an unorthodox approach to understanding the operations of the economy under capitalism. While this approach clearly has limited relevance to a socialist future, its observations and insights are relevant both to late-stage capitalism and to the process of transition to a new economic structure.

8.1 Modern Monetary Theory

Modern Monetary Theory, or MMT, is an approach to understanding capitalist economics, particularly in nations enjoying full monetary sovereignty – that is, nations which issue and have full control of their currency (such as the UK and US). Some countries have less control over their currency because they have borrowed heavily in another currency, or pegged their exchange rates or given up their national currency altogether in order to join a super-national currency such as the Euro. The following discussion refers to monetary-sovereign nations, like the UK, US, Canada, Australia and so on, but could also make sense if applied to the Eurozone (as a currency-issuing entity), given sufficient political co-operation among member states.[232]

Despite the strength of opinion to be found all over social media, most of us are not professional economists and would do well to leave the technical differences between complex economic models to those better placed to judge. However, there are good reasons for looking at MMT from a layperson's perspective here. Firstly, it's a serious and important current in contemporary economic discourse backed by a growing number of economists. Secondly, it adds to the ranks of economic theories which assert that it's possible for governments to compensate for the deficiencies of the market without plunging the economy into recession. Thirdly, it provides a number of interesting observations about the way we view economic issues, which are thought-provoking, even for those who may ultimately remain unconvinced by the wider project. Finally, MMT theorists often advocate a policy approach which is related to the proposal which we'll discuss in Chapter 9. (The MMT version shares the same basic principles and root as the policy I'll advocate, though they differ both in substance and purpose.)

MMT takes issue with the traditional understanding of the economy, in which government spending is financed by taxation and borrowing. According to the conventional view, when we look at the economy we see currency circulating around among individuals and businesses, undergoing various transactions – purchases, payments of wages and so on. Most transactions are taxed, such that a percentage is diverted from the recipient to the government which then – so the story goes – uses that money to provide infrastructure and other public services. According to conventional wisdom, the government runs its budget in the same way as a household. If it spends more money than it has received in taxation, then it has to borrow the difference and is in *deficit*, which is a 'bad thing'. If it is frugal and spends less than it receives in taxes, then the government is running at a *surplus*, which is a 'good thing'.

MMT economists challenge this picture. They point out that the government puts the money into the economy in the first place, the money circulates around, and with each transaction a percentage is taxed out and finds its way back to the treasury. Eventually most of the money finds its way back. The only money that doesn't is that which ends up either in savings accounts or leaving the country – as payment for imports or nestling in offshore tax havens. The difference between the money the government spends and the money it taxes back – the deficit – is the money it leaves in the economy. It's the money we – the population – have in our bank accounts, or have spent on shiny things from foreign countries. (In which case we have the shiny things.) MMT economists prefer to take a rounded view of the whole economy – the government deficit is the people's surplus. (Let's not get carried away and start thinking that the 'people's surplus' is some kind of community dividend – it's still distributed with depressing inequality.) The point here is that a government deficit isn't a bad thing or a problem to be solved. It's money currently held by individuals and businesses. MMT economists want us to think of the economy as comprising the government *and* individuals and companies, and to recognise that a government 'deficit' is just a term for money being in one part of the economy and not another.

This view has implications for the much vaunted idea of a government surplus too. Politicians of all colours like to promise that they will run the economy 'in the black'. At the 2019 General Election in the UK, the Liberal Democrats made a manifesto commitment to always run the economy at a surplus.[233] Conventional wisdom finds this approach very responsible and comforting. MMT says it's no such thing – that we should be horrified at the idea. What the Liberal Democrats (and other pro-surplus politicians) are saying is that for every billion pounds they spend into the economy, they'll be taxing more than a billion back out. Where is this extra money going to come from? How will we pay more in tax than there is? Collectively, as individuals and companies, we'll be going into debt to finance a government surplus. A government surplus is not a 'good thing' – it's just a term for money being in one part of the economy and not another – and the part that it isn't in is our wallets and bank accounts.

From this point of view, the national debt – the cumulative total of every year's deficit – is merely a record of the money the government has spent into the economy and not taxed back out. It's the money in circulation in society, in pension plans and savings accounts – at home and in offshore tax havens. Some of it is also money that's been spent on imports and found its way to foreign shores that way. We'll look at the implications of international trade balances shortly, but first we should look at a more immediate consequence of national debt – interest payments. While the government is in debt, it must meet interest payments on that debt. Some MMT economists argue that the government could (if it wished) avoid this by simply paying off the debt. How will the government afford such a policy? By printing currency, of course! If at this point you're picturing Weimar wheelbarrows and alarm bells are ringing at the thought of solving problems by printing money, you're not alone, but don't panic – everything is okay![234] MMT does have an unconventional approach to the control of the volume of money in the economy, but we're not in that territory yet. Printing money to pay off government debt doesn't necessarily have any inflationary effect. The majority of government debt consists of loans from the private sector in the form of bonds – sometimes called *Gilts* in the UK, or *Treasuries* in the US. But in effect, bonds are merely a different type of currency – currency which bears interest. In *The Deficit Myth* Stephanie Kelton suggests we think of bonds as 'yellow dollars' – they are essentially currency, very much like the green dollars in people's wallets.[235] When the government needs to raise money it prints 'yellow dollars' and effectively sells them to the private sector which pays for them with standard currency green dollars. Along with the 'yellow dollars' the private lenders get a promise that the government will pay them interest at regular intervals for a set period, and will then buy the yellow dollars back with green dollars.

Now, if the government was to decide tomorrow that it didn't like being in debt, then it could print several billion standard green dollars or pounds or yen or whatever and buy back the 'yellow dollar' bonds. (Obviously, no one actually prints money for these transactions now – they're just numbers in a database – but the 'yellow dollars' analogy works better if we imagine piles of cash!) The Federal Reserve or the Bank of England or Bank of Japan would then destroy the bonds and the impact on the amount of currency in circulation would be zero. Green dollars have been printed, but an equivalent amount of 'yellow dollars' have been destroyed. Swapping green dollars for 'yellow dollars' (bonds) has no impact at all on the net wealth of the private sector or the volume of currency in the economy, and therefore does not create any inflationary pressure. In fact, there may be a small deflationary effect because the government doesn't now have to pay interest into the economy to the bond holders.[236]

Perhaps the fear of inflation is overblown anyway. The real inflationary danger lies in the initial creation of bonds. When bonds are created the government 'prints the yellow dollars', swaps them out to gain green dollars from the commercial sector *and then spends the green dollars into the economy*. So now both the green dollars **and** the yellow dollars are in circulation, the volume of wealth in the economy is increased and the inflationary risk has been taken. And what's more the government is now committed to paying out interest until the loans expire, and then buying the bonds back at the end of the term – and both of these actions will be financed by...you guessed it – printing more bonds. This process goes on all the time – that's why the national debt is so high – but inflation remains low. So perhaps the relationship between the money supply and inflation isn't as straightforward as conventional economic wisdom would have us believe?

MMT economists accept that there is an inflationary risk associated with increasing the volume of money in the economy, but contend that the risk is absent when spending is directed at utilising otherwise under-utilised resources. One of the most obvious under-utilised resources in modern capitalist economies is the labour power of unemployed or under-employed people. Conventional economists argue that there is an optimum level of unemployment for the economy, and by this they *do not* mean zero unemployment. Neither do they mean just enough unemployment to allow fluidity in the labour market. The 'optimum' level is generally referred to as the NAIRU (Non-Accelerating Inflation Rate of Unemployment), and represents the amount of unemployment which (securely employed) economists and politicians deem to be acceptable. In theory the NAIRU is the lowest level of unemployment below which inflation would be expected to rise, but in practice a cottage industry is maintained consisting entirely of economists explaining why the expected relationship between inflation and unemployment hasn't materialised, or why action should be taken anyway despite the current unemployment level being higher than the NAIRU. But whether or not the NAIRU is a valid concept in modern economics, it's one that is widely used. It forms one-half of the 'dual-mandate' approach, in which governments charge their central banks with balancing inflation against unemployment, moving base interest rates up or down to achieve just the right balance.

In the US the NAIRU has been as high as 10 per cent, but is currently around 5 per cent, in the UK it's hovered at just under 6 per cent for most of this century to date, but rose to over 7 per cent in 2011.[237] Remember this is not *the actual unemployment rate*. This is the level of unemployment which governments decide is 'desirable'. If unemployment drops below this rate, action will be taken (usually in the form of raising interest rates) to slow the economy and raise unemployment. The reason for this is that low unemployment tends (theoretically) to lead to higher wages, which in turn leads to higher prices, which fuel demands for even higher wages and inflation begins to spiral out of control. (In practice this relationship has not been observed in recent decades, possibly as a result of developments like the gig economy, the return of zero-hours contracts, the increase in disguised employment and the drift from unemployment to under-employment.)

Kelton notes the human and social cost of this approach: 'To put it crudely, the Fed uses unemployed human beings as its primary weapon against inflation.'[238] But it's even worse than that. This grim reality becomes even more damning when we look more closely at what motivates such a policy. The decision to keep unemployment at or above a certain level is not made to prevent too much work getting done. It's not the *employment* that they're trying to limit, it's the *wages*.[239] Raising unemployment to stop people from working is just the mechanism – the functional goal is to stop them from having 'too much' money. Mainstream capitalist economics in the twenty-first century **requires 1 family in 20 to live in poverty.**

This point is driven home if we look at a statement to the House Committee on Financial Services from Jerome Powell, Chairman of the Federal Reserve: 'We need to have some sense of whether unemployment is high, low or just right.'[240] Now read that quote back, but replace *'unemployment'* with *'poverty'*: 'We need to know whether *poverty* is high, low or just right.' Mr Powell has clearly never spent a bus ride home from work worrying about whether the electricity bill might be waiting for him on the doormat when he gets home. Or had to choose between feeding the kids and paying the rent. If those charged with fine-tuning the economy believe that *not enough poverty* is a problem to be addressed, then it really is time to move on from the capitalist economic structure.

The fact that joblessness and poverty are government policies makes it even more galling that government-friendly media outlets encourage the jobless to blame immigrants or imports for their plight, and encourage the employed to demonise the jobless as idle scroungers. For those lucky enough to escape unemployment, the rise in interest rates increases the burden of mortgage debt and the cost of borrowing. At the lower end of the wealth spectrum, way below the point where mortgages become an option, short-term borrowing is often unaffordable and unavoidable at the same time. While a nudge in interest rates might appear a prudent move in the comfortable surroundings of the Bank of England or the Federal Reserve, the effects on the finances – and the lives – of low-income families can be catastrophic. And all to maintain a policy which hasn't been seen working for decades.

MMT economists propose a different approach. Since investing in the economy holds no inflationary risk as long as the investment is spent on bringing under-utilised resources into play, there is no reason why the state cannot institute full employment through a *jobs guarantee*. This policy does exactly what it says on the tin. The government sets a wage at which it will employ anyone who needs work, establishing a public option in the labour market. As long ago as 1943 economist Abba Lerner suggested that the government should encourage the private sector to get as close as possible to full employment, and then to use both monetary and fiscal policies to eliminate the last pockets of unemployment altogether.[241] Some MMT economists have suggested that the focus of such work should be caring for people, communities and the planet.[242] Some have used the expression 'employer of last resort'.[243] The details can be worked out once the principle is accepted. But first, MMT theorists need to win the argument about how the economy actually works and why spending constraints on currency-sovereign governments should be measured in terms of the real needs and resources of the people. They need to overcome the one-eyed view of the economy that sees only the government deficit and not the non-government surplus. The jobs guarantee, as understood and promoted by MMT theorists, is a mechanism with the laudable and civilised aim of delivering *sufficiency* to the majority of the population of a currency-issuing capitalist nation. As we noted in Chapter 5 there are some issues with the goal of providing sufficiency (though it's certainly an improvement over widespread *insufficiency*) and in Chapter 8 I'll look at how a variant of the jobs guarantee could be a significant step forward in the march onwards out of the capitalist economic structure and towards more meaningful and lasting benefits. First, though, there are a few more things to note about the MMT approach to understanding the economy.

Demographics and Automation

A jobs guarantee policy doesn't quite reach the entire population, but those able to work and their dependents would constitute a majority. In order to deliver sufficiency to the entire population a range of schemes for helping the young, old, ill and infirm, as well as those in education and training, would need to accompany the programme for full employment. As demographic change in most Western capitalist societies is set to shrink the proportion of working-age adults in the population, we'll need an economic approach able to mobilise the available resources to address the most pressing needs. A care-focused jobs guarantee scheme could be an important component of that project – co-ordinating our response to both the increasing demand in the care sector and the impact on the employment market of the impending wave of AI driven automation we discussed in Chapter 3. In terms of automation, and the potential to reduce the demand for labour, it's important to note that the jobs guarantee approach loses none of its effectiveness if demand for labour falls. The problem the jobs guarantee solves is not that people are spending too little time working, it's that they have too little money to spend. Guaranteeing 20 hours a week is as good as guaranteeing 40, providing the participants are being paid enough to live on. A large public-sector involvement in the labour market could help to overcome the usual upshot of automation under capitalism – the unemployment and destitution of part of the workforce while the rest work themselves into an early grave. With the scheme aimed at providing work and a living wage, the benefits and burdens of automation could be more reasonably shared.

International Trade

MMT theorists approach a country's international balance of payments in much the same way as they approach the government deficit. A trading deficit with another country simply means that they have some of your currency and you have (or have had) some of their goods and services. What has happened is that workers in, say, China have toiled to produce goods which have then been sent to, say, the UK, for consumers to enjoy. That's not such a bad deal – they did the work, we have the things. In return the Chinese now have a pile of sterling, which they can either hoard or spend back into the UK economy, creating demand and therefore employment opportunities. If China chooses to hoard that sterling, they'll probably convert it to government bonds (gilts, or 'yellow pounds' if you like), and the UK government will need to pay interest on those bonds. In pounds sterling. Which China can then hoard, or spend back into the UK economy – and so it goes on…

The real problem with such a deficit is that buying goods produced in China, for example, directly supports jobs in China, not in the UK. But with a jobs guarantee policy, that problem stops being a problem because the jobs lost will be replaced by other jobs, focused on the quality of life in society, rather than the production of consumer goods. I should add here that the jobs our trade deficit supports are often not the jobs we should be wanting to support. (If people want to buy goods at sweatshop prices and don't want to work in a sweatshop, then effectively they're requiring their government to run a trade deficit. The deficit isn't the problem with this – it's the sweatshop economy that's the problem.) If we can mature large sections of our economies beyond the profit motive, we'd be able to provide better quality employment, as well as better quality products, leading to a reduction in the volume of both employment and products we would require.

Free Money

An interesting development as MMT has gained exposure outside of university economics departments is that a misrepresentation of one of its central arguments has become common currency among both its lay-supporters and its critics. While some enthusiastic supporters address any government spending conversation with the maxim that a currency-issuing nation can never run out of money, opponents mock the 'magic money tree' approach and point, predictably, to the well-worn examples of Zimbabwe and Weimar Germany. The fact is that neither of these positions contains the whole truth.

Of course, currency-issuing governments cannot 'run out of money', they are always able to print more. But the inability to print more money was never the problem – it's the potential implications of doing so that are the concern. Conventional economics says that you need to raise taxes before you can spend, or if you borrow money to spend then you need to raise taxes to repay the loans and interest. MMT theorists say that this is back to front – you can't tax money out of the economy until after you've spent it into the economy, so taxation is not how you raise money to fund government spending. But that doesn't mean that currency-issuing governments can just print and spend infinite amounts of cash – just that the limits to what can be spent are real-world limits, not financial limits set by tax revenues. When those real-world limits are reached, though, what actions do MMT theorists suggest to stop the economy from overheating? Well, pretty high up on the list is raising taxes – not, now, to fund spending, but to balance the economy following government investment. So instead of taxing to spend, governments tax to balance the effects of spending. Either way, critics argue, if you want more hospitals you're going to end up paying more tax. The difference, essentially, is that MMT provides an approach to government investment which allows for both more generous spending and more informed control. Because the spending is determined by unused capacity, rather than cautious economic forecasts, there's likely to be more of it. And because adjustments are made in regard to actual economic events, rather than being made largely in advance using models of worst-case-scenarios, they can be calculated with greater certainty and therefore timed and targeted more effectively. From a non-specialist perspective, the upshot of the observations of MMT look, in the end, quite a lot like the familiar Keynesian idea that it's okay to direct resources into improving peoples' lives.

8.2 *Transforming Wealth*

Although Thomas Piketty writes from a more orthodox background, his proposals are in many ways more radical than those often proposed by MMT economists. In Chapter 6, I argued that the philosophical case for private ownership of the means of production is defunct. In *Capital and Ideology* Piketty similarly argues, albeit from a more practical angle, that the entire concept of ownership must be reconsidered if we are to attain the goal of a just society, suggesting that, 'In no region has enough attention been paid to transcending private property in its current form.'[244] Piketty is clear that there is no empirical basis for considering the institution of private property to be compatible with a just society. Drawing on his historical research he asserts that, 'The idea that strictly private property exists and that certain people have an inviolable natural right to it cannot withstand analysis.'[245] The accumulation of wealth is always the result of social progress, which depends on social infrastructures, the division of labour, the accumulation of knowledge and so on. Piketty is not merely declaring the current distribution of property unjust – his argument is that the concept of permanent, bequeathable ownership rights is untenable in a just society.

Once we are free from the shackles of the ideas that both the current distribution of resources and the institution of private ownership itself are sacred, a whole new world of possibilities opens up for us. Piketty grasps the nettle and recommends a radical programme of tax reforms – radical because they are not merely aimed at redistributing income, but at transforming the configuration of wealth – both who holds it, and *what it is*. He aims to make wealth ownership *temporary* through the circulation of property. The chief means of achieving this would be an annual wealth tax, a substantial inheritance tax and the introduction of a universal capital endowment, such that all citizens would receive a sizeable sum from the state on their twenty-fifth birthday. The idea of a universal capital endowment is not new – Thomas Paine argued for such a payment in *Agrarian Justice* in 1795.[246] More recently, Anthony Atkinson has promoted a similar plan, like Piketty combining it with a proposal for Universal Basic Income. The schemes suggested by Paine and Atkinson, though, are substantially less radical than that favoured by Piketty – both in terms of volume and in the scope of their transformational power. Paine suggested an endowment of 15 pounds for each individual, upon reaching the age of 18, equivalent to around £10,000[247] and Atkinson endorses a similar proposal.[248] While such schemes would be welcomed by most 18-year-olds (and many of us well past that age[249]), they constitute an income boost, rather than a transformative redistribution of wealth. Twenty-thousand pounds will pay off less than half the debt most students graduate with, it might be enough to start a small business, or to help with living costs during an apprenticeship, but it's not going to make significant inroads into the iniquitous distribution of productive resources which we identified in chapters 5 and 6 as the real problem facing us today. Piketty makes (and costs) the case for a universal capital endowment of €120,000 for every French citizen at the age of 25 – a figure equal to 60 per cent of average wealth. Financed by taxes on wealth and inheritance this intergenerational redistribution would have a significant impact on the distribution, not only of income, but of wealth, and potentially of capital – of ownership of the means of production. The universal capital endowment has other benefits, as it not only broadens the number of people who inherit wealth, but also improves both the timing and the predictability of their 'inheritance'. The average age of wealth holders would also be reduced, injecting energy and vitality into the economy.

Such a scheme still does not fully deliver the equality of ownership that we could call real socialism, but it goes a long way towards breaking the capitalist monopoly whereby wealth is permanently hoarded by a tiny minority, while the rest of us scramble for whatever income we can get. By taxing wealth annually, as well as on its transfer when it's bequeathed to heirs, and then providing each citizen with more than the current average holding, the ownership of a large proportion of productive assets becomes temporary, fragmented and distributed across the population, and across generations. Getting this kind of policy in place would require us to have begun to break down the idea that wealth has accrued to those who deserve it – that the historical record provides some kind of justification for the current distribution of ownership. But the implementation of such a policy reinforces the new paradigm, and could help to entirely transform our understanding of property and of *what ownership means* – moving us ever closer to our goal of a just distribution. To be clear – I don't think the implementation of a universal capital endowment (even of the scale envisaged by Piketty) is the answer to the problems caused by the capitalist economic structure. However, such a plan would help to fragment long-established capital holdings and see us very much closer to a mindset more accepting of policies which really could move us beyond capitalism.

As ever, Piketty's plan is fully costed – employing what he refers to as the 'progressive tax triptych' he takes aim at income, wealth and inheritance. While acknowledging that the details would need to be worked out through democratic deliberation in each case, he provides a template to illustrate the principle, using tax bands calculated on levels of wealth and income compared to national averages rather than fixed currency values. Perhaps the most striking element is the scale of universal provision made possible even with tax rates which are quite unremarkable, in the context of twentieth-century capitalism. Piketty proposes rates of 60 to 70 percent on wealth and income more than 10 times the national average, and 80 to 90 per cent on those over 100 times the average – levels entirely consistent with those in the strong growth economies of the UK and US between 1930 and 1980. This, he calculates, would raise a sum equivalent to 45 per cent of national income from income taxes (and a new carbon tax) which would be sufficient to finance the welfare state including health, education, pensions and a basic income. The wealth and inheritance taxes would raise a sum equivalent to 5 per cent cent of national income which would be used solely to fund the universal capital endowment.[250] A universal capital endowment of the scale envisaged by Piketty would be a step in the right direction, but doesn't deliver a socialist economic structure. Piketty's work illustrates just how much wealth has been hoarded by those in the higher percentiles of the economy – enough (if distributed with any kind of egalitarian impulse) to provide a start in life to every citizen. Instead, those representing the interests of the wealthy argue (as we saw above) that unless a fifth of families live in poverty there will be too much money in the economy. Piketty clearly demonstrates that there's quite enough money – it's just not well enough distributed.

9

Beyond Capitalism

He wants no servants under him,and no boss above his head
Bertolt Brecht, 1934[251]

9.1 Levelling the Playing Field

In our discussion of Modern Monetary Theory in Chapter 8, we looked at the concept of a job-guarantee scheme as a means of making the capitalist economic structure more civilised by encouraging widespread sufficiency and thereby reducing poverty. What I propose here is a version of the job-guarantee scheme, but with important caveats aimed, not only at alleviating *insufficiency of income,* but also at removing the structural disadvantages created by the iniquitous distribution of wealth and resources under capitalism. Taken in conjunction with the other measures we'll discuss later in the chapter such a programme has the potential to transform – over time – the nature of the bourgeois-proletarian relationship, and to contribute to the transition away from the capitalist economic structure.

In order to understand the best approach to moving away from private ownership of productive resources we need to be clear about the reasons for wanting to do this in the first place. The root of the problems we've identified throughout this work is that under capitalism most people enjoy no meaningful ownership of any means of production. As such, while they are free to sell their labour power on the open market, to the highest bidder (in contrast to pre-capitalist producers who enjoyed no such freedom), they are also *unfree* in that they are compelled – on pain of destitution – to sell their labour power to some capitalist or other. (Capitalist claims that this arrangement is not an infringement on the freedom of proletarians are addressed – and dispatched – in Chapter 6.) This necessity means that the value of the reward received by the worker is generally the product of an inequitable negotiation, and therefore less than would otherwise have been the case. Imagine a worker, with a small trust fund, for example, which provides sufficient income for a modest lifestyle, with the basic trappings required to participate in the social, political and cultural life of the community. A person thus furnished is unlikely to find sufficient appeal in the wages and conditions offered by many employers at the lower end of the labour market – in that position would you get out of bed at 4am to clean toilets in an office block for £6.45 an hour? Employers negotiating with workers in this position would need to offer a higher salary than if they were negotiating with workers whose only options were to work or starve. The difference between the levels of salary offered in each situation is a product of the proletarian's non-ownership of any means of production, and the size of this difference is a measure of the degree of exploitation suffered as a consequence of that lack of ownership.[252] We do not need to accurately measure this amount, or even to be confident that it is measurable, so long as we can agree that it's larger than zero.

This disadvantageous employment contract – this exploitation – which arises as a result of the concentration of ownership of productive resources in the hands of a tiny proportion of the population has long been the target of socialist and Marxist attention. The only way to end exploitation, it has usually been argued, is to remove this situation of concentrated ownership – and thus the corresponding widespread situation of non-ownership. The orthodox Marxist solution is to end exploitation by seizing the means of production from the bourgeoisie, by force if necessary. But why don't we try approaching this problem from the opposite direction? Perhaps, instead of seizing the means of production in order to end exploitation, we could take exploitation out of the equation and watch private ownership of the means of production (largely) wither away? (Or at least, lose much of its exploitative potential, and thus most of its appeal.)

The approach I'm suggesting here isn't simply to nationalise industries, but it does require a gradual extension of public ownership and responsibility – partly of new resources and partly of existing resources currently under private ownership. There is precedent for extensive nationalisation by a democratic government – in the post-war period in the UK, for example. Despite claims to the contrary in the right-wing press, the project had many successes, the NHS being the most obvious. Even though it is now being rolled back, it was hugely successful at its height – and its demise is rooted in ideological opposition to its existence, not in failures to provide an effective healthcare solution. Experience around the world shows us that public ownership is a perfectly reasonable and successful model for health, social care, education, water, power, libraries, roads, bridges, railways, the military and a host of other sectors. The important thing to understand is that in the scheme I propose, nationalisation isn't the goal but a side-effect of the process. It's not happening for its own sake, or because of some abstract ideological goal – or only in sectors where no one can make a profit. In this scheme it's happening *specifically to provide an alternative for the worker other than to sell their labour power to a capitalist enterprise, because it is the lack of that alternative which is the root of the iniquitous negotiating position in which workers find themselves*. Supporters of capitalism waste no time in explaining why nationalised industries can't compete with the free market to meet complex and changing consumer demands – so let's not.[253] Let's compete with private corporations *in the labour market*, not on the supermarket shelves – at first at least.

There's no shortage of work that needs to be done, but is not currently being done. In the UK we have shortages in the health and social care sectors, in infrastructure maintenance, in education and so on. We desperately need a large-scale programme to build huge numbers of affordable houses. Alongside these needs, there is a large amount of work being carried out for the public sector by private companies. Care homes and nursing agencies are an obvious example, but there's a long list of operations which used to be carried out perfectly reasonably by publicly employed workers which are now farmed out to the private sector, from running laundry services for hospitals to provision of military housing and catering.

Getting things done isn't the rationale for the scheme, though, nor – in our case – is reducing unemployment for the sake of it, though those are obviously both worthwhile achievements. For our purposes, we must go further than the usual conception of a job-guarantee scheme. The programmes recommended by MMT economists such as Bill Mitchell and L. Randall Wray refer to the government's role as that of 'employer of last resort'[254] while Anthony Atkinson recommends the system should provide work at minimum wage,[255] but for our purposes this isn't sufficient. If we want to address the structural basis of exploitation, we should push for the public sector to become the *employer of best practice*. If the government offers a fair wage, excellent working conditions, 6-weeks holiday a year, decent sick-pay arrangements, maternity and paternity leave and more, then the private sector is going to need to up its game to attract workers, particularly at the less well-rewarded end of the labour market. This isn't something that could happen overnight, but would need to be introduced in stages, beginning with existing positions and vacancies in the public sector, as described above. Over time the scheme would be expanded to encompass more and more sectors and skill levels. The point is for publicly-owned, operated or supported bodies to compete with capitalism not in the consumer markets, as was the case with experiments like Thomas Cook or British Airways, but to compete with capitalist enterprises as the employer of choice. Without the need to keep shareholders furnished with dividends public employment enterprises could afford to offer employees much better conditions than their private-sector counterparts. A viable, well-paid public-sector option in the labour market also levels up the playing field in the private sector as it means that workers can enter into employment negotiations from a less disadvantageous position – it could almost remove the need for minimum wage legislation because there would always be a better rewarded option than a minimum wage job in the private sector.[256] In itself, this doesn't redistribute ownership of the means of production to a wider population, but it does alleviate the exploitative consequence of that relationship, which is that workers must sell their labour power on disadvantageous terms. In doing so, this approach also makes ownership of the means of production less profitable – those accustomed to sitting back and watching the profits roll in will find their incomes on a consistent downward trend. Such a policy would necessarily lead to an increase in publicly-owned resources – and it's important to note that public ownership doesn't have to equate to centralised state ownership or control. Public bodies can be local in the way that housing authorities used to be in the UK, or specific to a sector, such as the erstwhile *Central Electricity Generating Board*. Or they could be both local and sector-specific such as *Transport for London*. Worker-owned co-operatives are not strictly in the public sector, but have the potential to play a huge role in breaking down the concentration of ownership of the means of production. From the Mondragon Corporation, a federation of worker co-operatives, now with over 80,000 members and operating in 150 countries to Cooperation Jackson democratising employment in Mississippi, there are existing, successful models to provide inspiration and guidance.[257] In the UK, we often neglect to notice that John Lewis Partnership (JLP) is also owned by its 80,000 employees, who receive a dividend pay-out each year of up to 20 per cent of their annual salary. The partnership, which owns a finance company and some small textile operations as well as department stores and the Waitrose supermarket chain, is run by a trust which is obliged to operate in the interests of its present and future staff.[258] The success of these – and other – co-operatives demonstrate that the bourgeois conception of ownership isn't the only game in town. It's likely that we won't know the final shape of such things until they emerge – as with the rise of capitalism, the process will involve many false starts and dead ends, and will continually evolve to meet new circumstances. We should look to incorporate and build on the work of theorists such as Michael Albert and Robin Hahnel who have proposed new ways in which co-operatives might play a central role in the democratisation of the workplace, and in replacing the failures of the labour market we identified in Chapter 7.[259] Albert and Hahnel develop a system of *participatory planning* intended to show that a third option exists between the market and central planning – a possibility denied by the likes of Milton Friedman. (Of course, it's undeniable that a third option exists between the market and central planning as such a position is witnessed daily in certain sectors of every mixed economy in the world, but Albert and Hahnel go further, claiming that their model can replace the conventional (non-participatory) market across the entire economy.) While proposals of this kind are valuable in working through problems of principle and practice, my feeling is that such blueprints are unlikely to reflect the full picture that will emerge as we move beyond the model in which the market is the final arbiter of value in goods, services and labour. Our concern, for now, should be to identify – and fight for – policies that have a transformative effect on the economic structure, such as the *employer-of-best-practice jobs guarantee* outlined here.

This approach has numerous advantages over the kind of piecemeal fettling with tax rates and employment conditions which we currently see – centred around minimum wage levels, in-work benefits and so on:

- The tasks people are employed to undertake are driven by actual community requirements, rather than their ability to generate profit for shareholders – the work that's being done is work that needs doing!
- It would be possible to use guaranteed-hours contracts, which provide flexibility for the worker without the precarious and uncertain nature of zero-hours contracts.
- By not being motivated by maximising profit for shareholders this kind of employment can promote a healthier work/life balance.
- Automation (including AI) can at last be welcomed as the benefit it should be, not the spectre it has become.

9.2 From Employment to Empowerment

By taking the job guarantee embedded in the Green New Deal programmes being promoted by democratic socialists in the UK and US, and simply adding the caveat that the government should aspire to be the first choice for employees, not the last resort, we transform the focus from employment to empowerment. By providing the offer of a genuine, well-rewarded and authentically useful job opportunity this scheme causes a significant shift in the employee-employer relationship in the private sector and forces private companies to pay for labour at its actual value. In effect, what this does is to remove the imbalance which is the source of the employer's margin of exploitation. No one's private property has to be seized and no one has to storm the Winter Palace – we can take a giant step in the direction of a post-capitalist economy with the minimum of friction.

There are parallels here to the creation of the NHS in the UK. Private practice wasn't outlawed. Private property was not commandeered. Instead a better option was provided by the state – it quickly became a beloved institution and for generations virtually no one used private healthcare. The fate of the NHS also provides a warning. Steps forward must be protected. Moves away from capitalist free-market economics need to be structural in nature – otherwise (if they're purely political or financial) they will be vulnerable to recapture by bourgeois interests, just as the NHS has been. (In the UK the NHS is so popular that politicians who want to privatise it have to claim that they won't privatise it, but will boost its funding and that they will build new hospitals and train more staff. Almost no one, including the privatisers, expects the private sector to be able to match the NHS for service.)

As with the NHS, the state taking on the role of employer of best practice will still leave room for private enterprise – particularly in cutting edge industries where innovation and responsiveness to consumer demand are key, but those are far fewer than we might imagine. Over time the basic and middling needs and wants of society would be more and more met by a range of publicly-owned and worker-owned projects. Moreover, we would be putting the economy into a state fit for the coming revolution in work practices so that the next wave of automation might deliver leisure and a better quality of life, rather than unemployment, destitution and rising inequality which is the stock response of capitalist economies to technological advance.

The free market will still exist (for now at least), but – for the first time – employers will need to pay employees what they're really worth. (What's left of the private sector should also be subject to at least the kind of worker representation – at board level – which is already a legal requirement in Germany and Sweden.)[260]

Capitalists who insist that the market should be the final arbiter should have no problem with this plan. All we're doing is simulating one dimension of the situation which would exist if all resources had at some point been fairly distributed. To argue against that would be to concede that the market can only work its magic if a tiny minority have first seized almost all of the means of production. That's the opposite of the story the capitalists like to tell – they have always claimed that they ended up with everything as the result of a fair competition. They can't now admit that the system only works because they already had possession of all the stuff at the outset. Entrepreneurs like to call themselves wealth-creators and job creators – the engine room of the economy, without whom we would all starve. Well, let's see it, then. If they – not workers – create wealth, then this scheme should present no obstacle to their continued success.

Of course there will be objections. Where will the money come from to offer such advantageous pay and conditions to workers? What will the effect be on prices in the private sector when companies have to pay higher wages to attract staff? These concerns are often (*always*) raised whenever a proposal is made to improve the lives or working conditions of employees. These prophecies of doom, however, never seem to come true. The concerns are regularly, and cynically, couched in terms of the effect on jobs – that higher wages means higher costs, which will inevitably lead to unemployment. That won't wash when the measure they're trying to oppose is the creation of better jobs and guaranteed employment.

Will prices of consumer goods increase? Well, they might. If they do – if they become more expensive once labour is rewarded at a fair price – that suggests that they've been under-priced before. Some products might prove unsaleable at the price they would have to be sold for. They would drop out of the market through lack of demand at the new price point. That happens all the time under capitalism, so defenders of that system can't object on principle to this consequence. (At least, not without admitting that their objection is based solely on their own interest. Such a position would require them to argue that their interests should come before the payment of a fair wage. If the demand for a product disappears once it's priced at its real cost, then why would capitalists mourn its loss? Aren't they supposed to love this kind of market mechanism?) Perhaps the nine-bladed disposable razor will never see the light of day. Consumers might have to get by on half a dozen different brands of laundry detergent. In return, we might fill most, or even all, of the hundred thousand vacancies in the social care sector. We might even be able to increase staffing levels to provide a better service. Over time – with decent training plans – we might even see the NHS fully staffed, and our crumbling infrastructure renewed.

Many of these aims are nothing new, and neither are they – in theory – unattainable under capitalism. But the nature of capitalism is that many of these needs can only be addressed to the extent that we restrict the operations of the free market. Such measures never go far enough and are always vulnerable to future reversals. The free market might be great for fine-tuning production to address the demands of the darkest corners of the matrix of money-backed spending habits, but it's a dismal failure at meeting the basic needs of post-scarcity society – employment, healthcare, social care, education, dignity for the most vulnerable and least able.

Joseph Stiglitz has imagined a similar scenario on a global scale, though only – I think – in an illustrative sense. He's argued that the rules of globalisation are also set to benefit the rich. They force countries to compete for business. This drives down taxes (and regulation) on corporations and weakens labour rights, environmental and health provisions and so on. 'Imagine what the world might look like if the rules were designed to encourage competition among countries for workers. Governments would compete in providing economic security, low taxes on ordinary wage earners, good education and a clean environment – things workers care about. But the top one per cent don't need to care.

Or more accurately, they think they don't'.[261] On a global scale we can only imagine, but at a national level such a scheme is entirely within our reach.

In our discussion of MMT in Chapter 7, I noted that any job-guarantee scheme would need to be complemented by provision for those not able to participate in employment. The idea of a UBI has gained ground in recent years, particularly during the Covid pandemic. Although UBI may provide an appropriate response to such an emergency, I'm not convinced of its suitability as a permanent measure. If we believe in socialism, and in achieving it by democratic means, it follows that we believe that a reasonable person – the English legal system's *man on the Clapham omnibus*[262] – would find life in a socialist economic structure to be more appealing than life under capitalism. Our task is to convince them of that fact in advance – politically speaking, we need to bring currently cynical populations with us. As such we need to focus on policies which are already popular (and there are a number of those) or for which we can make a straightforward case with clear benefits. Presented in isolation, the idea of a Universal Basic Income sets alarm bells ringing for many potential supporters, as it plays into the hands of a common – though inane – right-wing trope that socialism amounts to handing out free money to idle scroungers. Although UBI is more popular now than it's ever been, it tends to perform well in polls where the question misleadingly mitigates its universality.[263] In polls where universality is properly represented, support is both lower and more tentative.[264] Many people are justifiably concerned that UBI would exacerbate the perceived free-rider problem that already exists with welfare benefits while, at the same time, diverting resources to those who don't need them. Supporters of UBI, meanwhile, argue that universality is crucial – usually on the grounds that means testing is not only costly, but all-too-often punitive and discriminatory. A job-guarantee scheme heads off concerns about the free-rider problem usually associated with welfare benefits, but nevertheless a proportion of the population are not able to work for one reason or another. A basic income system is an appropriate mechanism for those in education or training, the elderly and infirm, those caring for children or other relatives or only able to work part-time and so on. Of course – once we attach conditions to the receipt of basic income it ceases to be *universal* – but we can live with that, particularly as those excluded would be in full-time employment, earning a living wage. (Effectively if they were to receive UBI, their payments would merely take the form of a tax rebate. The admin required for UBI for these workers seems unnecessary solely to honour the principle of universality, given that it would be trivial to make the necessary income tax adjustments to arrive at the same results.) Basic income for those where paid employment is not appropriate would replace any number of complicated and means tested benefits. While eligibility for such payments wouldn't need to be means tested, there is no reason why some eligibility criteria relating to personal circumstances could not be applied. (A no-questions-asked initial period of Basic Income payments, permissible every so often, combined with reasonably broad eligibility criteria, should provide sufficient cover for those for whom paid employment is not a suitable option at a given time.)

9.3 Health, Housing and Education

I noted above the parallels between the idea of the public sector as the employer of best practice and the introduction of the NHS in the UK. In both cases the conversion to a more socialist system is achieved by the creation of a public offering with which the private sector cannot compete. If we can rescue the public provision of healthcare from the privatisation zealots, and deliver a superior public offer of employment we'll be well on the way to a socialist economic structure. The obvious next steps are to extend the same principle to the public provision of housing and education. By providing better options than the private sector can offer in employment, health, housing and education we can improve fundamental aspects of most people's lives and push back the influence of the private sector and the iniquities it fosters.

Although the NHS is a service, rather than a strictly *productive* resource, it represents a huge asset in terms of public ownership (of property, buildings, equipment and so on), employs over a million people and accounts for around 10 per cent of GDP.[265] The social care sector is around a fifth of the size of the NHS and should be incorporated into it and benefit from increased investment.

A public house-building programme is desperately needed in the UK and many other countries. We need to invest in training in the building trades and to provide decent quality houses at affordable prices. New housing projects should be designed with sustainability, quality of life and community cohesion as priorities. A key issue in the UK housing crisis is that families who for years have been paying, for example, £1000 a month in rent often find themselves ineligible for a mortgage on the grounds that they might not be able to meet the monthly repayments of £800. The solution is to allow people to rent affordable public housing and when their payments total an amount sufficient to cover the cost of building a new house, those payments are converted to mortgage payments and the tenants become owners. The accumulated payments are then used to build another house and the cycle continues. A house swap system would permit people to move to other houses on the programme if they needed to upsize, downsize or relocate. There would be zero risk of default, because the house is rented until the payments are completed. Terms would be considerably shorter than the traditional 25-year-model because the interest rate wouldn't need to cover a profit margin for the lender and because the largest single cost of a house is the land with planning permission. As the public sector controls the permission, they largely control the cost of this significant aspect of the build. (If this sounds like an overly ambitious plan, remember over 5 million council houses were built in Britain between 1945 and 1980, of which £40 billion worth was then privatised over the next 25 years.[266] It's also worth noting that until the Thatcher era, a lot more land in the UK was in public ownership than is now the case. Brett Christophers estimates that the land privatised since 1979 accounts for 10 per cent of the British landmass, at a value of over £400 billion.[267] There's nothing unprecedented about the scale of the land purchase or house-building programme I propose.) This scheme wouldn't preclude the public sector from providing homes for sale and/or rent under traditional terms, or require legal intervention in the property market such as rent controls. Rent controls are a way of dealing with the problems caused by capitalism. Public-sector housing is a part of the move away from capitalism. Its appeal is similar to the idea of a job-guarantee programme where the public sector becomes the employer of best practice – here the public sector becomes the best landlord a tenant can have. Without commandeering housing stock for reallocation, or outlawing buy-to-let, or imposing rent controls we can make landlordism unattractive to property speculators. (There is something to be said for rent controls and so on, but only as means to mitigate against the ills of capitalism – here we want to be more ambitious than that.)

The involvement of the public sector in education varies significantly from country to country, particularly in post-compulsory provision. Despite state subsidies, the private education sector already prices itself out of the reach of most people – its exclusivity is part of the appeal to the 7 per cent who currently use it. While it may be unrealistic to attempt to provide a similarly luxurious education for all, we should at least aim to match the teacher numbers and class sizes currently available to privately educated children. Further and Higher Education should be available on the basis of ability, not ability to pay, but ought to be part of a wider programme of education and training focused on lifelong learning providing academic, vocational and recreational outcomes. Thomas Piketty notes that in France (for example – it's unlikely to be an outlier in this sense) public sector educational investment varies from 65,000 Euros to 300,000 Euros per person, over their lifetime.[268] An educational investment fund for each citizen might be a way to address the inequality here, as well as bringing more aspects of vocational training into the public domain. Increasing spending on schooling up to age 16 will also help to reduce the investment inequality – directly because those who are currently under-funded are largely those who leave school at 16, and indirectly because it should result in a wider constituency staying on to pursue Further and/or Higher Education. The details of educational funding can be worked out by democratic deliberation, informed by expert knowledge, but the principle should again be that the public sector needs to provide an offering of sufficient quality as to render the private-sector offering unattractive to most people.

With these four key areas of people's lives – employment, education, health and housing – rescued from the free market and offered to all citizens as high-quality options from the public sector we can begin to see the broad outlines of a post-capitalist future. The investment required to accomplish these goals will necessarily involve a greater degree of ownership and control of the means of production by bodies accountable to the public – central and local government, school boards, housing authorities, worker-owned enterprises and so on.[269]

As well as providing the most favourable option for employment, housing, education and healthcare, it clearly makes sense to extend public ownership to essential services (which are often also natural monopolies), such as energy, water and telecommunications. The road networks in most advanced countries are already largely publicly owned (though often privately constructed and maintained). A co-ordinated, publicly-owned, managed and maintained transport system including roads, rail, buses and trams is another area where public ownership and coordination can easily provide a better outcome than private competition for the busy routes and neglect of the rest of the network. The private sector can remain in place, for now at least, but with a much-reduced role in the provision of the fundamental requirements of life in the twenty-first century.[270]

Conclusion

So, to recap...

We have established (in Chapter 1) that it can be useful to view different societies throughout history in terms of the meaning of property and ownership in various times and places, and that as technology advances, different systems of ownership arise and persist when and because they encourage progress, and decline and are replaced when they become a drag on further development. We've noted the gradual, organic nature of this process of change. We've surveyed real-world examples of this process in the emergence of capitalism from European feudalism (Chapter 2), and we've looked at twenty-first century capitalism and concluded that it's nearing its expiry date – that it's materially outmoded (Chapter 3).

We examined the ideology of the capitalist era and found that the familiar axis of left-right politics still makes sense providing we view capitalism and socialism as consecutive phases in a continuum from tradition, custom and superstition to modernity, rationality and reason. (Chapter 4). We noted that capitalist ideology is founded on demands for certain equalities, but that these bourgeois equalities are not sufficient for the free and civilised society to which we aspire (Chapter 5).The capitalist claim that the system of private ownership enhances freedom has been exposed as logically inconsistent, and we've found any claims that the current distribution of resources is a just distribution to be without basis in logic or historical fact. We concluded that private property is incompatible with each of the socialist goals of freedom, justice and equality (Chapter 6).

In Chapter 7 we examined attitudes to work and its relationship to reward and innovation as well as to leisure and other non-productive aspects of life – and we found the labour market to be an ineffective mechanism for allocating what work gets done, who does it and how much they should be paid. We noted the observations of economists writing from an MMT perspective as well as those of Thomas Piketty, who I've described as having a more orthodox approach than MMT economists, but presenting more radical recommendations. We considered the ideas of Universal Basic Income and Universal Capital Endowment and considered the latter to be more valuable, while still belonging really to the transition to socialism, rather than its ultimate attainment (Chapter 8). Finally, in Chapter 9 we outlined a policy proposal whereby a public employment option would be made available to anyone who needed it, on terms designed to undermine the exploitative elements of the labour market. Although this proposal is not far removed from the state 'job-guarantee' scheme proposed by MMT theorists (among others) there is a crucial difference which, I contend, addresses a fundamental socialist objection to capitalism – that the workers, owning no means of production, are compelled to sell their labour power on disadvantageous, exploitative terms. By providing employment which is remunerated above the market rate, the policy of the public sector as *employer of best practice* drains the exploitative opportunities out of the capitalist economic structure. As well as requiring increasing public ownership[271] of the means of production, this approach fundamentally alters the exploitative potential of those productive assets that remain in private hands. In addition, this system enables us to address the problems of deciding which work needs doing and who is going to do it via a mature and responsible process, attaining a degree of progress far beyond the best the labour market has to offer. The principle of challenging the private sector not on the supermarket shelves, but in the labour market – simply by being (for many) the best available employer – can be adapted for health and social care, housing and education. The public sector can provide the best option for housing and employment as well as for health and education.

The system of private property upon which capitalism is built diminishes freedom, widens inequality and is reaching the point where it hinders progress. It's time to move on – the process is already underway.

Afterword

The Politics of Change

The proposals I've outlined in Chapter 9 focus largely on measures related to production, the economy and the provision of the fundamental requirements of contemporary, everyday life. But one of the reasons why achieving these things seems so far away – particularly given that they are generally quite popular with electorates – is that our political systems are fundamentally broken, so we'll also need to address some of the problems with those systems and look at ways in which we can improve things.[272] What political changes would help us to achieve the transformational policies we advocate? What should politics look like in a socialist – or even a transitional – economic structure?

The first and most basic improvement (in the UK, US and Canada at least) is switching to a democratic electoral system. The case for doing so is beyond reasonable doubt, though the details are still up for discussion.

Democratic Elections

The UK, US and Canada all need to join the twenty-first century and adopt democratic electoral systems. The case had been made extensively for around half a century so I'll only offer a brief recap here. General Elections in the UK and Canada and elections to the House of Representatives in the US (as well as numerous local and state/province/territory elections in each of these countries) use the *First Past the Post* electoral system (FPP), which is fundamentally flawed in terms of delivering a democratic result. Electoral systems for elections to assemblies such as the House of Commons or the House of Representatives or a county council or state legislature have one role – to translate votes into seats. First Past the Post fails to do this. It's important to note that even if electoral districts (constituencies in the UK) each contained exactly the same number of voters, FPP would not produce democratic results. In fact, numbers often vary wildly[273] and boundaries are subject to incessant political manipulation (This manipulation – *Gerrymandering* – is a serious problem under FPP. Proportional Representation (PR) renders constituency boundaries politically irrelevant, so we can go back to having them drawn with reference to actual communities, instead of twisted for party advantage.) Although it's uncommon that one party gains the most votes and a different party wins a majority of seats (but it can, and does, happen[274]), every election under FPP produces a distorted result. The 2019 election in the UK, for example, produced an unassailable majority of 80 seats for the Tory Party despite 56 per cent of votes going against them. That FPP is undemocratic is beyond doubt.

There are numerous democratic systems in use around the world, but the one I think is most suited to the UK, US and Canada is not currently used anywhere, but is closely related to one proposed by the Hansard Society in 1976, and not too dissimilar to that in use in New Zealand.[275] This system is astoundingly easy to understand and to implement. The election is conducted exactly as it is currently, with each voter casting a single vote in their constituency, and the candidate with the most votes winning that seat in the House. Additional members are then added to the House, until the proportion of MPs for each party reflects that party's proportion of votes. Additional members are not drawn from a party list but are the closest losing candidates from constituencies the party in question didn't win. It's that simple.[276]

The same system can be adapted for any election to an assembly – local, state, national, federal – democracy is actually a very simple mechanism. The complicated part is overcoming the propaganda of the opponents of democracy and winning an election under the current, undemocratic system. In the UK, the obvious path is an electoral alliance, where only one pro-democracy candidate stands in each constituency – probably from the party that performed best in that constituency in the most recent General Election. Win the election, institute PR and call another election. Next stop – an elected 'Upper' Chamber to replace the affront to democracy known as the House of Lords.

This system can work in the US for the House of Representatives, and local and state legislatures – it's an obvious move forward. The case for reforming presidential elections and the Senate is less clear cut. Although there are some terrible arguments put forward in defence of the Electoral College, a case can be made which is plausible (if unconvincing) and as such should be addressed. The (only sensible) case for the Electoral College is the same as the justification for the Senate – that the US is a union of states and that the states, not just the citizenry, deserve recognition and representation. To what extent do people identify with Wisconsin or Texas before they identify with the US? If most, or even very many, put state before nation, then there's a case for a system that balances the interests of the citizenry with those of the states. (Or, if you prefer, balances the interests of the citizenry of the US with the interests of the citizenry of each state.) Looking in from the outside I can see the formal validity of the argument, but also that the current arrangements appear massively tilted in favour of the states over the citizenry. If the Senate is to remain – as a representative of the idea of the union of states – then its role should be greatly diminished – perhaps in line with the House of Lords in the UK, which can only delay, not throw out, legislation, and has no say at all on finance bills. As for the presidency, a more acceptable approach would be to use some kind of transferable vote or ranked choice system. This is also true for any elections where a single person will take office – elections for presidents, mayors and so on can only benefit from a ranked choice system of some kind. Such systems are common in the democratic world, they help to ensure that people wielding executive power are at least palatable to a majority and facilitate the emergence of new parties as people can signal support for a candidate outside of the mainstream without wasting their vote.

Finally, a democratic electoral system will always produce an assembly which reflects the votes of the electorate, and often this will mean coalition government. To reflect the collaborative nature of the political process in a democracy, the parliament buildings of many countries are arranged in a horseshoe formation, rather than in the dualistic, combative arrangement found at the House of Commons in Westminster (where the distance between the two front benches is (incorrectly) said to be just over two sword lengths to stop the protagonists from duelling). As well as the layout, the size of the chamber is inadequate – there aren't even enough seats for all the MPs – and the surroundings are far too much like a dining-hall at a private school, which is presumably why the procedures so often resemble a juvenile bun fight. The UK needs a new, purpose-built parliament building (preferably away from London) and new set of conventions and procedures which encourage politicians to behave as if they're at work. The scenes in the House of Commons are a national embarrassment. People live or die depending on what's decided in the House – let's stop treating it like a game for noisy, overgrown schoolboys.

Political Education

We should also try to improve the calibre of members of the House – the current crop of MPs, with a few notable exceptions, are not people who should have any role in running a country in the twenty-first century. It's not feasible to set entry requirements to the House of Commons – the electorate are entitled to elect whoever they wish. It's not unreasonable to expect members to undergo some in-work education and training, though – at a basic level for MPs, with some advanced, subject specific courses for ministers. Although the civil service is supposed to provide the expertise to complement the ministers' political outlook, it surely wouldn't hurt for housing ministers to have a grasp of human geography and urban planning philosophies, or – to cite a recent example – for the Equalities Minister to have heard of the *Marmot Report*, the key document on health inequalities.[277] In addition to competence, we should be able to expect integrity from our representatives, which will require a major overhaul of the expenses system as well as civil penalties for misconduct leading to disqualification from holding public office. (Any socialist party worthy of the name should have such measures embedded into its own organisational practices and not need to have them imposed from above.) Although it's probably impossible to close all avenues for illicit political funding (in the short term, at least) we can begin with strict (and low) limits for donations, and a democratic overhaul of funding arrangements for political parties and candidates through a system of personal funding vouchers, where each citizen receives an annual voucher to donate to the party of their choice.[278]

The low bar for entry into the political class is partly a product of the poor quality of public discourse surrounding political issues and this situation is a barrier to the proliferation of socialist ideas. The more informed about politics people are, the less vulnerable they become to manipulation. To counter this, a programme of political education is necessary. I'm not talking here about any kind of indoctrination or propaganda. What I'm referring to is simply some basic coverage of fundamental aspects of the political system – how elections work, the different roles of (and relationships between) the government, Parliament and the judiciary, the spheres of influence of Westminster and the devolved parliaments, and various local government entities. Should MPs be delegates or representatives? How do parties work? A basic, neutral course on how our political institutions work would help to protect people from propaganda – would arm them with a basic understanding which would help to protect them from manipulation. I'm talking here about the kind of things that a socialist – and even a transitional – political system ought to aspire to, rather than the thorny issue of *how* we should go about organising to achieve those aims. That problem has been ably addressed by authors such as Micah Uetricht and Meagan Day (*Bigger Than Bernie: How We Go from the Sanders Campaign to Democratic Socialism*[279]), Bhaskar Sunkara (*The Socialist Manifesto – The Case for Radical Politics in an Era of Extreme Inequality*[280]) and Jeremy Gilbert (*Socialism in the Twenty-first Century*[281]), and of course this is also an ongoing discussion. Here I will only comment on the question dividing the left in the UK – the supposed play-off between socialist principles and electability.

The UK Labour Party is undergoing an attempt to work out how to become electable, and is going about this in entirely the wrong way. The centrists' familiar refrain that there's no point having principles unless you have the power to implement them is countered by the left's response that there's no point having power if you don't use it to further your principles. The essential difference between the two wings of the party is that for the centrists the goal is power and the principles are an inconvenient obstacle to attaining that goal. For the left, on the other hand, the goal is a better society and the need to win power is the inconvenient obstacle.

So – how do we go about winning power, while retaining our principles? Not by running endless focus groups and trying to chase votes by adopting whatever is popular, that's for sure. We know that a core set of socialist policies are popular and so should focus on those. At the same time, Labour must be realistic about the chances of winning an election in its own right under the current, undemocratic electoral system. While the 40 per cent of the vote share in Labour's 2017 defeat was considerably more than that achieved in 2005 for Tony Blair's last victory (35.2 per cent), the distribution of votes left the party with 93 fewer seats than in 2005, and nowhere near a majority. The rise of the Green Party and the SNP (particularly given the SNP's geographically concentrated support) has almost certainly sent us beyond the window in which Labour could win an outright majority. An electoral alliance against the Tories and the UKIP/Brexit/Reform continuum with the introduction of PR as the single objective is the first step in the process of regaining the leftward momentum that was lost in the late seventies, and which has seen us slip ever backwards in the intervening years.

The Labour Party must accept that its primary purpose is to improve the lives of the most vulnerable in society, rather than to pursue single-party government. Unfortunately, though, this principle is not universally acknowledged by Labour MPs or members. We noted earlier Jeremy Gilbert's observation that the dividing line in British society between those who want to see decisive, structural change and those who do not runs right through the Labour Party. The party urgently needs to split into the two parties it really should be – perhaps really should always have been. The problem is that these two factions are forced into a single party by the undemocratic nature of the UK electoral system. Before any such split can happen, we need to have a democratic electoral system. Once that's achieved, I think the split would be inevitable, and would be a broadly positive move. Instead of a bitter winner-takes-all fight inside the old party, each of the new parties can concentrate on persuading voters of the value of its programme. It's entirely possible that a genuinely socialist party could win enough seats in a democratic election to be able to hold at least some influence in a coalition government. Many on the left view any coalition as a compromise, but we should see it as an opportunity. One or two redline policies as a condition of entering the coalition, and perhaps a front bench seat or two. This gives socialist politicians ministerial experience, provides an opportunity to show that socialist policies are workable and affordable, that our politicians can act with integrity and insight – an opportunity to lead by example and to bring a currently unconvinced electorate on a leftward journey.

I've advocated programmes designed to undermine the exploitative aspect of employment, to remove precarity and to redefine the relationships between work and reward. These policies, and their outcomes, are not the end game – we can't see from here the exact details of what the post-capitalist world will look like. The ultimate goal is a transition to an entirely new understanding of ownership of the planet's resources – one that is centred on justice and sustainability, rather than growth and destruction.

Endnotes

1. FISHER, *M. Capitalist Realism – is there no alternative?* Zero Books, 2009. p1.
2. Most international institutions (the World Bank, WHO etc) use a wholly inadequate definition of poverty based on a measure anchored to a 'poverty line' set at an equivalent purchasing power of $1.90 per day at US prices in 2011. The US Department of Agriculture calculated that in 2011 the very minimum necessary to buy sufficient food was $5.04 per day, without counting other requirements for survival, such as shelter, healthcare and clothing or the ability to participate in civil society through education and access to information. Peter Edward has calculated a far more realistic 'poverty line' of $7.90 per day (in US 2011 dollars), which leaves over 47 per cent of the world's population in poverty. See https://www.gapminder.org/tools/#$state$time$value=2019;;&chart-type=mountainand https://www.theguardian.com/global-development-professionals-network/2015/nov/01/global-poverty-is-worse-than-you-think-could-you-live-on-190-a-day For hunger-related deaths see: https://www.un.org/en/chronicle/article/losing-25000-hunger-every-day
3. Is it true that capitalism was *ever* the optimum system for our needs? Only an extended discussion about the meaning of terms such as 'optimum' and 'our needs' can resolve this question and since the upshot has no bearing on the wider point that *even if it was, it no longer is* then that discussion would be redundant here.
4. More precisely, 28 per cent of the world's agricultural area is used annually to produce food that is lost or wasted: http://www.fao.org/news/story/en/item/196402/icode/ (See footnote 2 for hunger-related deaths).

5. World Economic Forum. https://www.weforum.org/open-forum/event_sessions/the-disposable-society
6. https://www.theguardian.com/business/2019/jan/21/world-26-richest-people-own-as-much-as-poorest-50-per-cent-oxfam-report
7. From a strictly capitalist perspective the question might be whether these inequalities are even problems which we should be trying to solve. As we'll see in Chapter 6, for some capitalist philosophers, any solutions to inequality necessarily come at the expense of freedom, and that price is not one they're willing to pay.
8. See Chapter 7 for details.
9. See GRAEBER, D. *Bullshit Jobs – the rise of pointless work and what we can do about it*. Penguin, 2018. p157.
10. The first draft of this introduction was written while Trump was in office. As I write this footnote (March 2021) he is again in the news, having started to hold rallies to reignite support for an as-yet ill-defined goal. Whatever the future holds for Trump, his toxic legacy will be with us for some time yet. (Trump was not the only factor in the decline in standards of political behaviour and discourse in recent years, but he was by no means *merely* a symptom, as some have claimed.) Johnson, meanwhile, somehow maintains his lead in the polls, while presiding over a catastrophic response to the pandemic, an array of assaults on established constitutional checks and balances and a booming market in crony contracts unprecedented in scale or effrontery.
11. MMT is a set of observations rather than a set of policies, but policy recommendations do emerge from advocates of the approach.
12. HOBSBAWM, E. *How to Change the World: Tales of Marx and Marxism*. Abacus, 2012.
13. See for example

https://www.nytimes.com/2014/12/07magazine/who-wants-to-buy-a-politician.html
https://www.ft.com/content/d12f7f70-22a4-11dd-93a9-000077b07658
https://www.opendemocracy.net/en/dark-money-investigations/revealed-the-elite-dining-club-behind-130m-donations-to-the-tories/
https://www.theguardian.com/politics/2020/may/30/call-for-inquiry-into-why-senior-tory-robert-jenrick-helped-donor-avoid-40m-tax
https://www.huffingtonpost.co.uk/entry/boris-johnson-jenrick-westferry_uk_5ed7cbb6c5b6a4143c45db62
https://amp.theguardian.com/politics/2020/jun/25/minister-suggests-voters-could-raise-planning-issues-tory-fundraisers
https://bylinetimes.com/2020/09/21/government-ppe-deals-conservatives-364-million/

14. In 2019 Johnson made various attempts to roll back the English constitution to the seventeenth century by subordinating Parliament to the government. That the opposition to these measures was not limited to left-leaning, or even centrist, politicians is evidenced by his need at one point in the process to withdraw the whip from (effectively to eject from the Parliamentary Conservative Party) 21 Conservative MPs, including two former chancellors, seven other former cabinet ministers and Winston Churchill's grandson, Sir Nicholas Soames. In 2020 disgraced former Secretary of State for International Development and current Home Secretary Priti Patel joined Johnson by lending her weight to a long-running tabloid campaign to undermine the judiciary and the wider legal system, attacking 'activist lawyers' and 'lefty human rights lawyers and other do-gooders'. That such attacks on the legal profession should come

not only from the Home Secretary, but from official Home Office communications is unprecedented. https://www.theguardian.com/politics/2020/oct/25/lawyers-ask-johnson-and-patel-to-apologise-for-endangering-colleagues

15. See PIKETTY, T. *Capital and Ideology*. Harvard University Press, 2020. p16-17.
16. Although Trump has now been defeated at the ballot box, his poisonous legacy remains. Many are rightly critical of the lack of decisive action from the Biden administration, but there is nevertheless – still – a difference between Biden and Trump. Like Johnson in the UK, Trump's 'leadership' is characterised by an assault on the institutional gains of the modern era and an appeal to a backward-looking outlook, opposed to science, learning, knowledge and rationality. In comparison, Biden is a *business-as-usual* Democrat, doing little to move things forward, but not actively pursuing an imaginary golden age.
17. For it's largely an English, rather than British, phenomenon.
18. Under Clement Attlee, Labour won a landslide in the 1945 election and a further victory in 1950. The 1951 election saw Labour win a quarter of a million more votes than their rivals, but the undemocratic nature of the UK electoral system awarded the win to the Conservatives, installing Churchill as a peacetime PM at his third attempt.
19. Although Corbyn is no longer leader of the Labour Party, and Sanders failed to win the Democratic Party nomination in the US, their influence remains – both inside and outside of their respective parties.
20. Virtually no one has heard of the Kingdom of Aksum, which is exactly my point. It lasted four times longer than capitalism, and yet it's already an obscurity.
21. 'Productive forces' is the standard terminology in

Historical Materialist circles, but we needn't stand on ceremony here.

22. Although we may sometimes employ the legal terminology of 'ownership', this should always be taken to mean 'effective control', which is often, but not always, the same as legal ownership. For extensive justification of this decision, see COHEN, G.A. *Karl Marx's Theory of History – A Defence*. Princeton University Press, 1976. Chapter VIII.
23. Similarly, if this brief summary of the methodology and terminology of historical materialism feels abstract and somewhat academic, that's okay too. We're really just outlining a framework – once we begin to map these concepts onto actual historical processes and social phenomena, they will start to make more sense, and their relevance will become more apparent.
24. COHEN. G.A. (1976). The Development Thesis states that *the productive forces tend to develop through history*, and that they will do so because humans are sufficiently capable and rational, in the relevant sense. The claim that the productive forces *tend* to develop claims more than that they *have* developed – it requires that development is more than a collection of happy accidents. It is in the nature of the forces to develop, and that nature derives from human inventiveness and rationality. Cohen also notes that the Development Thesis says *less* than that the productive forces have developed, because it does not require that they always develop, or even that they do not sometimes regress. The Primacy Thesis states that *the nature of the production relations in a society is explained by the level of development of its productive forces* to a far greater extent than vice versa. This means that the character of the social aspect of the economic base (who owns what in a society) is largely explained by the material aspect – the

level of technological development. As well as allowing for a degree of feedback from the relations to the forces, Cohen introduces the mechanism of *functional explanation* in order to accommodate the interaction between these two elements. In this way his approach permits an explanatory flexibility in understanding Marxist interpretations of historical explanation. The Dobb-Sweezy debate in the 1950s and the 'Brenner Debate'in the 1970s, for example, concern the details of what Cohen calls the *elaboration* of the mechanism he describes. (In much the same way that Darwin's ideas on natural selection by chance variation provide the *elaboration* of the mechanism of evolution.) The debates between those historians take place *within* the parameters of Cohen's mechanism – at least to the extent that they remain within the broad precepts of historical materialism. While those debates are interesting in their own right, the detailed discussions are beyond the scope of the current volume – a more general understanding of the mechanism at work will be sufficient here. Readers who wish to grasp the detailed historical arguments would do well to examine Harvey J. Kaye's *The British Marxist Historians* or the collection edited by Rodney Hilton, *The Transition from Feudalism to Capitalism*.
KAYE, H.J. *The British Marxist Historians*. Polity Press, 1984.
HILTON, R. (ed). *The Transition from Feudalism to Capitalism*. Verso, 1976.

25. COHEN, G.A. Functional Explanation: Reply to Elster. *Political Studies* Vol.XXVIII, No.1. 1980. p129.

26. It's important to note, though, that no one is suggesting that all development will cease. The technological revolution currently underway is providing incredible tools with which we can hopefully address many of the problems arising out of the transition away from capitalism, as well as many age-old problems which capitalism hasn't

been equipped to solve. It is the development of ever greater productive capacity that has been capitalism's strong point, and it is that capacity which is no longer the determining factor in our progress.

27. MEISKINS WOOD, E. *The Origins of Capitalism*. Verso 1999. p193.

28. PIKETTY, T. (2020) p154-155. Piketty includes the dominant ideology at work in a society as part of his classification and argues that a proprietarian ideology might prevail in pre-industrial societies with a traditional type of property holding, as well as in an industrialised capitalist society. In my schema such societies would be considered to be transitional structures between feudalism and capitalism.

29. The concept of the *invisible hand* originates with Adam Smith, who used it to justify inequality and self-interest on the grounds that this unseen force existed by which the outcome of a number of wealthy people acting selfishly would be the mystical arrival of some consequence that would benefit everyone. 'By pursuing his own interest he frequently promotes that of the society more effectually than when he really intends to promote it.' (SMITH, A. *An Inquiry into the Nature and Causes of the Wealth of Nations,Books IV-V*. Penguin, 1999). Over the years, the expression has evolved to encompass a wider meaning, summarised by Joseph Stiglitz as 'the idea that free markets lead to efficiency as if guided by unseen forces'. https://www.theguardian.com/education/2002/dec/20/highereducation.uk1

30. There's a parallel here with military technology. For most of history the human need for security – the society-level equivalent of the survival instinct – has provided the incentive to devise ever more efficient means of killing ever larger numbers of humans. But the advent of sufficient nuclear firepower to destroy the entire planet

several times over has put an end to that. There is no need to find ways of killing more people, more quickly than an H-bomb. The focus of military development has shifted towards other aspects of warfare – armour, accuracy, remote control, avoiding detection and so on. Of course, these avenues have always been a part of the whole picture (just as considerations other than volume have been part of commodity production), but just as maximum destruction is no longer the required focus of military development, 'more stuff' is no longer the required focus of our productive capacities.

31. WILKINSON, R. and PICKETT, K. *The Spirit Level – Why Equality is Better for Everyone*. Penguin, 2010.
32. WILKINSON, R. and PICKETT, K. (2010) p6.
33. VONNEGUT, K. *Breakfast of Champions*. Grafton, 1973. p22. (With minor adaptation.)
34. See OVERTON, M. *Agricultural Revolution in England – The Transformation of the Agrarian Economy 1500-1850*. Cambridge University Press, 1996. p63.
35. OVERTON, M. (1996) p135-8.
36. There's no suggestion that urbanisation or industrialisation were conscious aims of anyone at the time. But they are the processes that developed, and they could not have done so on the back of sixteenth-century outputs.
37. Obviously here I'm using the term *revolution* in its general sense of a significant change, not in the strict historical materialist sense of a transition from one economic structure to another.
38. This system was developed in Belgium and adopted in Norfolk and is often known as the Norfolk Four Course system.
39. The practice of sheep folding had existed before the development of the four-field system, but the introduction of grazing and fodder crops greatly increased its volume

and significance.

40. Here 'progressive' means technologically forward-looking, not socially liberal.
41. MEISKINS WOOD, E. *Liberty and Property*. Verso 2012. p212.
42. MORE, T. *Utopia*. Cassell & Company, 1901. p19.
43. Robert Bell, quoted at https://www.historyofparliamentonline.org/periods/tudors/monopolies-elizabethan-parliaments
44. STUART, J. *The Trve Law of Free Monarchies*. 1598.
45. The 'Glorious Revolution' is the name given to the coup which saw James II replaced by William III. James's Catholicism had been tolerated by the emerging bourgeois interest, largely on the grounds that on his death he would be succeeded by his Protestant daughter Mary and her husband, William of Orange (also James's nephew). Since Mary's birth, James had converted to Catholicism and, following Mary's mother's death, had married an Italian princess. On the birth of James's son in 1688 the prospect of a Catholic dynasty loomed. In addition to a potential return to the religious wars of earlier centuries, this raised the prospect of a revival of the doctrine of Divine Right, and also that Parliament would be involved in a power struggle against a king with the backing of France, Spain and the Vatican. The strength of parliamentary power by this point was sufficient to force James to flee and William and Mary were invited to take the throne as monarchs answerable to Parliament and whose power was constitutionally limited.
46. OVERTON, M. (1996) p143.
47. The extent of navigable rivers increased by 50 per cent between 1660 and 1720, over 15,000 miles of turnpike roads were laid in the eighteenthcentury; the canal network was expanded to play a significant role from the 1770s and the

growth of railways from the 1830s completed the picture. OVERTON, M. (1996)p142.

48. PIKETTY, T. (2020) p168. The situation in France was similar, with the émigré billion – a law of 1825 awarding over a billion francs of taxpayers' money to aristocrats as compensation for land lost in the aftermath of the revolution.
49. MARX,K. *Capital I*. Lawrence & Wishart, 1954. Chapter 28.
50. In *Liberty and Property*, Ellen Meiskins Wood argues that the effects of the Norman Conquest and the Reformation on British politics led to a more unified monarchy and landed aristocracy than in other European countries. This in turn led to unique relations between landowners and tenants which encouraged experimentation in agricultural methods. MEISKINS WOOD, E. (2012) p216.
51. PIKETTY, T. (2020) p86.
52. WRIGHT, G. *Slavery and Anglo-American Capitalism Revisited*. Tawney Lecture to the Economic History Society, Belfast, 2019. Available online at https://drive.google.com/file/d/1ZLLNGFiwtrjeza5oZwFQRG-J3MQdn1cP/view
53. McCLELLAND, P. and ZECKHAUSER, R. *Demographic Dimensions of the New Republic*. Cambridge University Press, 1982.
54. GALLMAN, R. E. 'Self-Sufficiency in the Cotton Economy of the Antebellum South' in PARKER, W.N. (ed.), *The Structure of the Cotton Economy of the Antebellum South*. Agricultural History Society, 1970. See also WRIGHT, G. (2019).
55. WRIGHT, G. *The Political Economy of the Cotton South*. W.W. Norton, 1978. p150-154. In Mississippi, for example, even after voting for secession in 1861, the Convention still voted against re-opening the slave trade.

56. While we're on the subject of a historical materialist approach to slavery in the US, it's worth mentioning a widely repeated myth about Marx's attitude to slavery and abolition. As would be expected, from both a moral and a historical point of view, Marx was vehemently anti-slavery and wrote to Lincoln in 1865 to congratulate him on abolition, but there's another letter from Marx – this time written in 1846 to Pavel Annenkov, which is often quoted to suggest that Marx saw slavery as inevitable, and as compatible with progress. The oft-quoted section, though, is clearly in fact Marx's (not entirely accurate) characterisation of Proudhon's position, not Marx's own view. Letter from Marx to Pavel Vasilyevich Annenkov, in MARX, K. and ENGELS, F. *Marx and Engels Collected Works(MECW)* Vol 38, Lawrence & Wishart, 1975. p 95. http://hiaw.org/defcon6/works/1846/letters/46_12_28.html

    Letter from Marx to Lincoln, *The Bee-Hive Newspaper,* No. 169, November 7, 1865; https://www.marxists.org/archive/marx/iwma/documents/1864/lincoln-letter.htm
57. MARX, K. (1954) p399.
58. MARX, K. *Capital III.* Lawrence & Wishart, 1959. p259.
59. MARX,K *and* ENGELS,F. *MECW. Vol. V.*p49.
60. Marx to Zasulich 8/3/1881. See MARX, K andENGELS, F. *MECW Vol. XXIV.* p370. Preface to 2nd Russian edition of the *Communist Manifesto* (1882), see MARX, K andENGELS, F. *MECWVol. XXIV.* p426.
61. MARX,K. (1954) p714.
62. MARX,K. (1954) p714.
63. 1905 Statistical Yearbook. See PUSHKAREV, S. *The Emergence of Modern Russia 1801-1917.* Pica Pica Press, 1985. p278.
64. KLEBNIKOV,P.G. *Agricultural Development in Russia, 1906-*

17: *Land Reform, Social Agronomy and Cooperation*. 1991. p 352 (PhD Dissertation, at http://etheses.lse.ac.uk/1141/1/U048311.pdf), and OVERTON, M. (1996) p77.

65. Tsar Nicholas abdicated in favour of his son Alexei, then changed his mind and re-abdicated, this time in favour of his brother, Grand Duke Michael, but Michael wasn't keen to take on the role and the Romanov dynasty came to an end – and with it the Tsarist regime. Michael's reluctance has been variously attributed to a respect for constitutional democracy or a fear of being assassinated.
66. Of these nationalities, 22 had more than a million members in the 1989 census, and 15 had their own republics within the USSR.
67. https://www.democracyatwork.info/acc_global_unrest
68. The two most frequently quoted passages from Marx in this respect both date from 1848. One is in a newspaper column about the revolution in Vienna, in which Marx's supposed assertion of the inevitability of 'revolutionary terror' should really (but usually isn't) be read along with the earlier part of the sentence in which it is stated that events 'will convince the nations that' [revolutionary terror is unavoidable]. This is an observation, not a recommendation. (See *Neue Rheinische Zeitung*, 136, November 1848. Available at https://www.marxists.org/archive/marx/works/1848/11/06.htm). The other passage – from the *Communist Manifesto* – is more straightforward: the proletarians' goals 'can be attained only by the forcible overthrow of all existing social conditions'.
69. Interview with *New York World*, July 18, 1871. Available online at https://www.marxists.org/archive/marx/bio/media/marx/71_07_18.htm
70. Speech to The International Working Men's Association on September 8, 1872, printed in *La Liberte*, September 15. Available online at https://www.marxists.org/archive/

marx/works/1872/09/08.htm

71. MARX, K. *Capital I.* p672.
72. MARX, K. *Capital I.* p676.
73. MARX, K. *Capital I.* p674.
74. MARX, K. *Capital I.* p668.
75. PIKETTY, T. (2020) p7.
76. PIKETTY, T. (2020) p66.
77. CLARK, J.C.D. *English Society 1688-1832*. Cambridge University Press, 1985. p4.
78. COHEN, G.A. (1980) p129.
79. PIKETTY, T. (2020) p8. For example, Meiskins Wood argues that the civil wars in England were fought between two competing interests for control over a unified state, whereas the revolutionary conflicts in Europe were often fought between interests which represented different components of a fragmented state. In both cases, though, capitalism emerged out of feudalism. See MEISKINS WOOD, E. (2012) p216.
80. COHEN, G.A. *Why Not Socialism?* Princeton University Press, 2009.
81. MARX, K. *Capital I.* p668.
82. https://www.theatlantic.com/business/archive/2013/03/how-wall-street-devoured-corporate-america/273732/
83. HUDSON, M. *Killing the Host – How financial parasites and debt destroy the global economy*. Islet, 2015.
84. STIGLITZ, J.E. *The Great Divide*. Penguin, 2015. p10.
85. PETTIFOR, A. *The Production of Money – How to break the power of bankers*. Verso, 2017. p8.
86. GALBRAITH, James K. *Inequality and Instability. A Study of the World Economy Just Before the Great Crisis*. Oxford University Press, 2012.
87. Affiliate marketing is the process by which people try to get credit for having delivered you to online retailers and are rewarded financially for doing so. Websites now use

tag management software which obscures the number of affiliates from the user, but when it was possible to view them using extensions such as Ghostery it wasn't uncommon for sites to rack up dozens of affiliate links per page.

88. https://www.telegraph.co.uk/films/0/does-world-really-need-15-harry-potter-advent-calendars-asked/
89. http://www.fao.org/news/story/en/item/196402/icode/
90. The 'decrease in wealth' for the bottom 20 per cent is actually an increase – a doubling – of debt. Figures from the Federal Reserve Survey of Consumer Finances (SFC). See https://www.federalreserve.gov/econres/scf/dataviz/scf/table/ and https://dqydj.com/net-worth-by-year/
91. The Luddites were impoverished textile workers in the North Midlands and north of England, active in destroying stocking frames and other machinery from 1811 to 1816. There's little evidence of a coherent political position – their actions were directed at the new technology which was putting them out of work. See, for example, PEEL, F. *The Risings of the Luddites*. Nabu Press, 2011.
92. Swing riots spread across the south, east and midlands of England in the 1830s. Like the Luddites, the Swing rioters were ostensibly opposed to new machinery that was suppressing wages, in this case threshing machines and other agricultural developments, but were also probably symptomatic of wider distress. Captain Swing – like Nedd Ludd – was a fictional, symbolic leader of the movement. See for example HOBSBAWM, E. and RUDE, G. *Captain Swing*. Phoenix, 2001.
93. Quoted in GRAEBER (2018) p157.
94. RUSSELL,B. *In Praise of Idleness*. Unwin, 1976. p21.
95. MURO,M. et al. *What Jobs are Affected by AI?* Brookings Institution, 2019.https://www.brookings.edu/research/

what-jobs-are-affected-by-ai-better-paid-better-educated-workers-face-the-most-exposure/
96. WEBB, M. *The Impact of Artificial Intelligence on the Labor Market*. 2019. Available at SSRN: https://ssrn.com/abstract=3482150.
97. GOLDTHORPE, J.H. et al. 'The Affluent Worker and the Thesis of Embourgeoisement: Some Preliminary Research Findings' in *Sociology*. 1967.
98. LOCKWOOD, D. The 'New Working Class' in *European Journal of Sociology*. Vol. 1, No. 2, (1960), p253.
99. PAXTON, S. (2021) p40-42.
100. See for example HODGES, D. The Intermediate Classes in Marxian Theory. *Social Research*, 23, 1961.
101. COHEN, G.A. (1976) p98.
102. RUSSELL, B. (1976) p99.
103. Within the relevant range of technological development.
104. RUSSELL, B. (1976) P17.
105. Other unautomatable jobs are available.
106. BASTANI, A. *Fully Automated Luxury Communism*. Verso, 2018.
107. WILKINSON, R. and PICKETT, K. (2010).
108. WILKINSON, R. and PICKETT, K. (2010).
109. PIKETTY, T. *Capital in the Twenty-First Century*. Harvard University Press, 2017. p305.
110. STIGLITZ, J.E. *The Price of Inequality*. Norton, 2013. p334.
111. STIGLITZ, J.E. (2013) p342.
112. STIGLITZ, J.E. (2013)p269.
113. Flying Patrol Group, 'It Breaks my Heart'. From *Get Heavy*. East Coast Road Productions, 1985.
114. FERGUSON, L.W. 'The Stability of the Primary Social Attitudes: I. Religionism and Humanitarianism'. *Journal of Psychology*. 1941, 12. EYSENCK, H.J. Sense and Nonsense in Psychology. Penguin, 1956. ROKEACH, M. *The Nature of Human Values*. Free Press, 1973. MITCHELL, B.P. *Eight*

ways to run the country: a new and revealing look at left and right. Greenwood, 2007.

115. By 'original left' here I mean the first time the labels were used, rather than the first time the ideas were promoted.
116. https://avalon.law.yale.edu/18th_century/declare.asp
117. As I mentioned in Chapter 1, the UK and US are – at the time of writing – regressing from this long-term overall progress, under a cloud of populist dogma harking back to a 'golden age'. Most forward-looking, modern, liberal democracies continue to make gradual progress in delivering political and judicial equality to their citizens.
118. https://soundcloud.com/poltheoryother/does-labour-face-terminal-decline-w-jeremy-gilbert
119. Since 1997 the Labour Party in the UK has required some local constituencies to select their candidate for a parliamentary election from a list containing only women. The percentage of female MPs in the House of Commons has risen from under 10 per cent in 1997 to 33 per cent now, with Labour reaching 51 per cent in 2019.
120. HAYEK, F.A. *The Road to Serfdom*. Routledge, 2001.
121. NOZICK, R. *Anarchy, State and Utopia.* Basil Blackwell, 1974.
122. COHEN, G.A. *On the Currency of Egalitarian Justice and Other Essays in Political Philosophy*. Princeton, 2011. p3.
123. See, for example, George Orwell's *Animal Farm* and the short story 'Harrison Bergeron' by Kurt Vonnegut in *Welcome to the Monkey House* – neither Orwell nor Vonnegut were fans of either capitalism or inequality, but their dystopian fiction has been used by defenders of capitalism as warnings against any attempts to address inequality. ORWELL, G. *Animal Farm*. Penguin, 2008. VONNEGUT, K. *Welcome to the Monkey House.* Harper Collins, 1972.
124. *Declaration of the Rights of Man and of the Citizen* (France, 1789):

https://avalon.law.yale.edu/18th_century/rightsof.asp *Declaration of Independence* (USA, 1776): https://avalon.law.yale.edu/18th_century/declare.asp

125. Cromwell's concessions included the restoration of the king to the throne before the arrangements for indemnifying the parliamentary soldiers or paying the arrears of their wages would be complete. The Levellers and other radicals didn't trust the king to honour either commitment, and more importantly wanted a more democratic settlement than that negotiated by Cromwell. Five of the most radical regiments elected *Agitators* who presented a new manifesto – *The Case of the Army Truly Stated*. This quickly morphed into a new pamphlet, a draft proposal for an English constitution – *The Will of the People* – which formed the basis of the case for radical reform and the starting point for the Putney Debates.
126. There's every reason to think that Cromwell was merely buying time until he was in a position to suppress the agitators, but Charles I's escape in November saw the resumption of hostilities and put the discussions of England's future on hold.
127. WOODHOUSE, A.S.P. *Puritanism and Liberty – Being the Army Debates (1647-49) from the Clarke Manuscripts with Supporting Documents*. University of Chicago Press, 1951.
128. WOODHOUSE, A.S.P. (1951) p53.
129. WOODHOUSE, A.S.P. (1951) p58.
130. WOODHOUSE, A.S.P. (1951) p58.
131. WOODHOUSE, A.S.P. (1951) p66.
132. FRANCE, A. *Le Lys rouge*. Calmann-Lévy, 1894. p.118. Many English translations mistranslate égalité not as *equality*, but as *quality*, which removes much of the point being made. For the original French, see https://fr.wikisource.org/wiki/Le_Lys_rouge/VII
133. COHEN, G.A. (2011) pviii.

134. SEN, *A. Equality of What?* The Tanner Lecture on Human Values, Stanford University, 1979. http://www.ophi.org.uk/wp-content/uploads/Sen-1979_Equality-of-What.pdf
135. See, for example, Thomas Paine: 'Charters have no other than an indirect negative operation. They do not give rights to A but they make a difference in favour of A by taking away the right of B and consequently are instruments of injustice'. PAINE, T. *The Rights of Man*. Isaac Eaton, 1795. p125. In a more recent incarnation, we might note that while John Rawls' conception of justice tolerates inequalities, such inequalities are required to be justified via the 'Difference Principle'. If full equality is not more just than lesser equality, there would be no need for such a position. (Of course, inequality may still figure in the package that turns out to be the optimal solution, but that's not because inequality is just, but because there are other goals in the world besides justice.) See RAWLS, J. *A Theory of Justice*. Clarendon, 1971.
136. RAWLS, J. (1971) p60.
137. COHEN, G.A. (2011) p44.
138. https://www.nytimes.com/2014/12/07/magazine/who-wants-to-buy-a-politician.html
https://www.ft.com/content/d12f7f70-22a4-11dd-93a9-000077b07658
https://www.opendemocracy.net/en/dark-money-investigations/revealed-the-elite-dining-club-behind-130m-donations-to-the-tories/
https://www.theguardian.com/politics/2020/may/30/call-for-inquiry-into-why-senior-tory-robert-jenrick-helped-donor-avoid-40m-tax
https://www.huffingtonpost.co.uk/entry/boris-johnson-jenrick-westferry_uk_5ed7cbb6c5b6a4143c45db62
https://amp.theguardian.com/politics/2020/jun/25/minister-suggests-voters-could-raise-planning-issues-

tory-fundraisers

139. NAGEL, T. *Equality and Partiality.* Oxford University Press, 1991. p5.
140. Nagel's progressive approach to the conceptual understanding of property with regard to taxation in *The Myth of Ownership* does not commit him to the idea that current distributive injustices are intolerable. See NAGEL, T. and MURPHY, L. *The Myth of Ownership: Taxes and Justice.* Oxford University Press, 2004.
141. Gini coefficient 33.7. https://worldpopulationreview.com/countries/gini-coefficient-by-country/
142. Gini coefficient 45. https://worldpopulationreview.com/countries/gini-coefficient-by-country/
143. FRANKFURT, H. Equality as a Moral Ideal. *Ethics Vol. 98, No. 1* Oct., 1987. pp. 21-43
144. PIKETTY, T. (2020) p976 and p985.
145. https://www.youtube.com/watch?v=3wj48ACMWeI
146. See for example the last section of MARX, K.(1954).
147. https://www.youtube.com/watch?v=lsWndfzuOc4
148. https://www.youtube.com/watch?v=TcEWRykSgwE
149. http://www.fao.org/news/story/en/item/196402/icode/
150. https://www.youtube.com/watch?v=DR2rYCxT0lg
151. https://www.youtube.com/watch?v=3wj48ACMWeI
152. Raphael Hythloday in MORE, T. (1901).
153. Writing during the Cold War, John Rawls always insisted that any just society must allow individuals to choose their own career path – even if elements of socialism were to be accommodated, a Soviet-style, centrally-dictated labour distribution was not to be tolerated. While this is a perfectly understandable position, it's telling that he hadn't noticed that many people in capitalist economies with a free market in labour still don't get to choose their own career path. Just because you're not being directed by some grey-faced bureaucrat, it doesn't mean that

you've made a free choice to spend 40 hours a week packing brake pads in a warehouse or collecting trolleys in a supermarket car park. Under capitalism a free choice of career is a luxury only a minority enjoy.

154. The existence of personally owned items which are also used in production does not render this distinction untenable. For a longer discussion of non-bourgeois ownership of the means of production see my *Unlearning Marx,* Chapter 2.2.

155. Around a third of workers – less than a sixth of the population – contribute to a pension fund. In the UK 10.4m have active private pension plans while there are 32.89m in employment, including self-employment. https://assets.publishing.service.gov.uk/government/uploads/system/uploads/attachment_data/file/836637/Personal_Pensions_and_Pensions_Relief_Statistics.pdf https://www.ons.gov.uk/employmentandlabourmarket/peopleinwork/employmentandemployeetypes/bulletins/employmentintheuk/april2020. We might also note that most people don't hold significant personal property either. Home ownership is often cited as a factor which makes people feel like stakeholders in the economy rather than bystanders, but again its importance shouldn't be overstated. The rental sector accounts for around a third of households in the UK and US (though can vary from 10-60 per cent of households in capitalist economies) and large chunks of homeowners' homes are actually owned by mortgage companies. (https://www.ons.gov.uk/peoplepopulationandcommunity/personalandhouseholdfinances/incomeandwealth/datasets/householddebtwealthingreatbritain). Any remaining equity is vulnerable to the requirements of social care in retirement, leaving most people in a precarious position with regard to their likelihood of bequeathing wealth to their descendants.

156. LOCKE, J. *Second Treatise on Government and A Letter*

Concerning Toleration. Oxford, 2016. p5 (§6).

157. HAYEK, F. (2001) p108.
158. BERLIN, I. *Four Essays on Liberty*. Oxford University Press, 1969. I piii and RAWLS, J. (1971) p239. The position taken by Rawls is somewhat more complex than the representation I have provided here, but the core fact still stands – that, for Rawls, however undesirable poverty may be, it does not constitute a lack of freedom or liberty, and so (being of a lower 'rank' than liberty) its rectification should not come at the expense of the liberty of others. Rawls argues that poverty does not diminish liberty, but 'the worth of liberty'. (p179).
159. The IHS is the bizarrely named Institute for Humane Studies, the kind of organisation which likes to present itself as a 'Think Tank', but which is more appropriately referred to as a lobby group, or simply a propaganda outfit.
160. ASHFORD, N. *Principles for a Free Society* (2nd ed.). Blomberg & Janson, 2003. p45.
161. https://inequality.org/facts/global-inequality/#global-wealth-inequality
162. My use of the word 'unnecessary' does not prejudge the answer to the question of justice in resource distribution. Whether or not the current distribution is just, these deaths ***are*** unnecessary.
163. https://www.theguardian.com/news/2002/jan/26/guardianobituaries.socialsciences
164. NOZICK, R. (1974) p151.
165. NOZICK, R. (1974) p149.
166. NOZICK, R. (1974) p149.
167. NOZICK, R. (1974) p169.
168. https://www.theguardian.com/money/us-money-blog/2014/sep/26/rich-work-harder-ceos-jack-ma
169. See previous footnote.

170. REICH, R. B. *The System – Who Rigged it, How to Fix it*. Alfred A. Knopf, 2020. p144.
171. https://www.forbes.com/sites/teresaghilarducci/2020/08/31/most-americans-dont-have-a-real-stake-in-the-stock-market/
172. SHRUBSOLE, G. *Who Owns England – How We Lost Our Land and How to Take It Back*. William Collins, 2019. p267.
173. Of the 37 OECD member countries, 32 impose higher taxes on earnings from labour than earnings from ownership of the means of production. (The exceptions are Chile, Mexico, New Zealand, South Korea and Australia.) For corporation tax rates see: https://stats.oecd.org/index.aspx?DataSetCode=Table_II1
For tax on income from labour see:
https://taxfoundation.org/publications/comparison-tax-burden-labor-oecd/
174. MARX, K. and ENGELS, F. The Communist Manifesto in COWLING, M. (ed.) *The Communist Manifesto: New Interpretations*. Edinburgh University Press, 1998. p25. (This volume features a new translation by Terrell Carver, from which the quote is taken.)
175. https://www.theguardian.com/commentisfree/2011/nov/07/one-per-cent-wealth-destroyers
176. https://web.stanford.edu/~pmitnik/EconomicMobilityintheUnitedStates.pdf
https://www.jrf.org.uk/sites/default/files/jrf/migrated/files/money-children-outcomes-full.pdf
https://jamanetwork.com/journals/jama/fullarticle/2513561
177. 'Moral merit' is actually Nozick's phrase but it accurately summarises the set of considerations Hayek rejects.
178. HAYEK, F.A. *The Constitution of Liberty*. Chicago University Press, 1960. p87.
179. In Oscar Wilde's *Lady Windermere's Fan* Lord Darlington remarks that a cynic is a person who 'knows the price of

everything and the value of nothing'.

180. NOZICK, R. (1974) p158.
181. STIGLITZ, J.E. (2013) p334.
182. STIGLITZ, J.E. (2013) p34.
183. In the UK, tenants pay – on average – 45 per cent of their income in rent alone, and as much as 75 per cent in London. See, for example, https://www.benhams.com/press-release/landlords-investors/how-75-of-income-required-to-rent-in-parts-of-uk/
184. PIKETTY, T. (2017). The average labour share of income in G20 economies is marginally over 60 per cent and most of that necessarily covers outgoings rather than accruing as wealth. https://www.oecd.org/g20/topics/employment-and-social-policy/The-Labour-Share-in-G20-Economies.pdf
185. OVERTON, M. (1996) p126. The total sown area of arable land in England in 1800 was 11.5m acres.
186. LOCKE, J. (2016) p15 (§25).
187. LOCKE, J. (2016) p15 (§27).
188. LOCKE, J. (2016) p16 (§27).
189. LOCKE, J. (2016) p17 (§31).
190. LOCKE, J. (2016) p25 (§46).
191. NOZICK, R. (1974) p178.
192. ROTHBARD, M. *The Ethics of Liberty*. New York University Press, 2002. p244.
193. LOCKE, J. (2016) p37 (§73).
194. LOCKE, J. (2016) p24 (§44).
195. NOZICK, R. (1974) p230-231.
196. The general principle, in most provinces, was that land held by a feudal title would be modernised. Feudal obligations such as *corvées* (labour dues) and *cens* (payment by military or other service) were converted to money rents (a process which had happened piecemeal in England and other European countries throughout the

sixteenth century. In most cases the tenant lost security and communal rights, while the landlord enjoyed the benefit of a money-rent which he was at liberty to increase at will, effectively gaining the power of eviction.) *Lods* (a tax due to the feudal lord on the transfer of property from one tenant to another) were largely replaced by a property transaction tax, payable to the state.

197. PIKETTY, T. (2020) p103.
198. LOCKE, J. (2016) p23. (§43).
199. PIKETTY, T. (2017) p305.
200. REICH, R. (2020) p141-142.
201. LOCKE, J. (2016) p18. (§34).
202. LOCKE, J. (2016) p20. (§37).
203. Rawls reserves judgement on the truth of this claim, but maintains that *if* it is true then it may be sufficient to justify inequalities. See RAWLS (1971) p68.
204. NOZICK, R. (1974) p178-179, including reference to Fourier's position according to Alexander Gray in *The Socialist Tradition*. Harper & Row, 1968. p188.
205. PAINE, T. *Rights of Man, Common Sense and Other Political Writings*. Oxford University Press, 1995. p419.
206. GALBRAITH, J.K. 'Let us begin: An invitation to action on poverty' in *Harper's,* March, 1964.
207. COHEN, G.A. (2011) p189-91. Wolff also refers to possibility as liberty and permissibility as freedom, but I think this distinction is unnecessary. Liberty and freedom are generally used interchangeably and there seems to be no precedent for, or value in, the connection of these terms separately to the concepts of permissibility and possibility.
208. WINSTANLEY, G. *The Law of Freedom in a Platform,* Benediction Books, 2009. (1652).
209. MARX, K and ENGELS, F. *Collected Works*. Lawrence & Wishart, 1975 (Volume XXIV). p85.

210. NOZICK, R. (1974) p160-161.
211. NOZICK, R. (1974) p154.
212. NOZICK, R. (1974) p160.
213. In Douglas Adams' *Hitchhikers Guide to the Galaxy* the Lintillas were clones whose numbers ran into the billions because the cloning device which created them had suffered a malfunction which meant that a new clone was already partially made before the previous one was finished, so it was impossible to turn the machine off without committing murder.
214. GRAEBER, D. *On the Phenomenon of Bullshit Jobs: A Work Rant* at https://www.strike.coop/bullshit-jobs/.
215. LOCKE, J. (2016) p15 (§27).
216. See https://millercenter.org/the-presidency/presidential-speeches/december-3-1861-first-annual-message
217. RUSSELL,B. (1976) p21.
218. GRAEBER, D. (2018) p240.
219. This is a moral position – I neither have nor require any proof or supporting evidence. If you disagree with this proposition, you're probably reading the wrong book.
220. If you're thinking that a dignified life isn't a luxury, you might like to broaden your frame of reference to include the 20,000 people who starve to death every day and the 47 per cent of the world's population who live in poverty. (See footnote 2 for references).
221. GRAEBER, D. (2018) p11.
222. GRAEBER, D. (2018) p6.
223. Of course, some of the resistance to implementing the recommendations of the inquiry stems from a reluctance to inconvenience the owners of such tower blocks, but in any civilised society public money would be made available to remedy a situation in which tens of thousands of tenants live in high rise tinder boxes. https://hansard.parliament.uk/commons/2020-09-07/debates/A97D95F3-

B6A5-423A-A820-6A8B28A8C189/FireSafetyBill

224. FORD, M. *Rise of the Robots – Technology and the Threat of a Jobless Future*. Basic Books, 2015.
225. KAPLAN, J. *Humans Need Not Apply: A Guide to Wealth and Work in the Age of Artificial Intelligence*. Yale University Press, 2015.
226. BRYNJOLFSSON, E. and McAFEE, A. *The Second Machine Age – Work, Progress, and Prosperity in a Time of Brilliant Technologies*. W. W. Norton, 2016.
227. COHEN, G. A. (1976) p198.
228. See NOVE, A. *Studies in Economics and Russia*. Macmillan, 1990. p303.
229. ADAMS, D. *The Hitchhikers Guide to the Galaxy Original Radio Scripts*. Harmony Books, 1985. p35.
230. FRIEDMAN, M. *Capitalism and Freedom*. University of Chicago Press, 1982. pix.
231. PIKETTY, T. (2020).
232. The complication here is that the Eurozone is not equivalent to the EU, so some member states of the EU retain their own currencies. Nevertheless, as a currency-issuing entity, some of the observations of MMT should apply to the Eurozone, even if the ability to act on such observations is reduced by a complex political situation.
233. https://www.libdems.org.uk/liberal-democrats-2019-manifesto
234. Hyperinflation in the Weimar Republic led to stories of wheelbarrows full of banknotes and thieves who tipped out the banknotes to make it easier to steal the wheelbarrow. Economists sometimes refer to hyperinflation as the *wheelbarrow problem*.
235. KELTON, S. *The Deficit Myth*. John Murray, 2020. p36.
236. Stephanie Kelton quotes economist Eric Lonergan's 2012 thought experiment in which he asserts that the Bank of Japan could pay off all its debts, leaving the private sector

holding the same value in cash as they had previously held in bonds. KELTON, S. (2020) p94.

237. http://ercouncil.org/2018/chart-of-the-week-week-49/ https://obr.uk/box/the-equilibrium-unemployment-rate/
238. KELTON, S. (2020) p52.
239. According to the supporters of the dual-mandate approach, the same upwards pressure on wages at the lower end of the scale would occur if the unemployed were paid an equivalent of a low-end salary in unemployment benefit.
240. Quoted in KELTON, S. (2020) p53.
241. LERNER, A.P. 'Functional Finance and the Federal Debt' in *Social Research*, Vol. 10.1 (Feb. 1943), p. 38-51.
242. KELTON, S. (2020) p64.
243. MITCHELL, W.F. and WRAY, L. R. *Full Employment Through a Job Guarantee: A Response to the Critics*, 2005. Available at SSRN: https://ssrn.com/abstract=1010149
244. PIKETTY, T. (2020) p103.
245. PIKETTY, T. (2020) p990.
246. PAINE, T. *Rights of Man, Common Sense and Other Political Writings*. Oxford University Press, 1995. p420.
247. A direct inflation calculation would suggest that £15 in 1795 is equivalent to £1800 in 2021, but agricultural wages (for example) averaged around 20 pence per day (excluding beer) in 1795, making £15 equivalent to 30 weeks' income (remembering that there were 240 pence in the pound until decimalisation in 1971). A 21-year-old on minimum wage now will make £9840 in that time. See http://faculty.econ.ucdavis.edu/faculty/gclark/papers/farm_wages_&_living_standards.pdf. Table 5, p17.
248. ATKINSON, A, *Inequality: What can be done?* Harvard University Press, 2018. p171.
249. ...and even many of us whose own children are well past that age.
250. PIKETTY, T. (2020) p983.

251. BRECHT, B. The Song of the United Front. 1934 (Translation from *The Songbook of the International Brigades* athttp://www.zisman.ca/InternationalBrigadesSongbook/IBSongbook2.pdf)
252. There is some debate as to whether the concept of exploitation in this sense is merely descriptive of the outcome of a disadvantageous position or if it implies that the stated misallocation is morally objectionable. Some Marxists argue that the logical analysis of the employer/employee relationship is better without a moral dimension – not, presumably because they think that there isn't one, but because they view it as muddying the waters – as distracting from a sound, logical argument. The moral case has been discussed in chapters 5 and 6. For the purposes of the present discussion let's just note that the proletarian enters into a disadvantageous contract because the lack of ownership of means of production allows for few realistic alternatives.
253. That's not to say we should concede that they are always right on this matter, but to advocate making a tactical decision to address this issue on another front.
254. WRAY, L.R. Modern Money in SMITHIN, J. *What is Money?* Routledge, 1999. MITCHELL, W.F. and WRAY, L.R. *Full Employment Through a Job Guarantee: A Response to the Critics*, 2005. Available at SSRN: https://ssrn.com/abstract=1010149
255. ATKINSON, A. B. (2018) p303.
256. Minimum wage legislation should remain so long as there's a private sector, but would become effectively obsolete once a public service position was available to anyone at a civilised salary.
257. See for example https://www.mondragon-corporation.com and https://cooperationjackson.org
258. In 1999 an employee suggested that JLP should be floated

on the stock market. The proposal was rejected by the trust's Central Council because selling it off for the benefit of current employees would clearly not be in the interests of future employees, who are also beneficiaries of the trust. (At the time, estimates of the partnership's value suggested that each employee's share was worth around £100,000.) See http://news.bbc.co.uk/1/hi/business/the_company_file/451620.stm

259. ALBERT, M. and HAHNEL, R. *The Political Economy of Participatory Economics*. Princeton University Press, 1991.
260. Since 1976 German firms with over 2000 employees have been required to reserve half the seats on the board (with voting rights) for workers' representatives. The requirement is one-third for smaller firms with over 500 employees. In Sweden a third of seats – and votes – must be reserved for workers' representatives in all firms of more than 25 employees. We can be more ambitious in this respect.
261. STIGLITZ, J. (2015) p93.
262. The 'man on the Clapham omnibus' is an expression in English law, meant to personify the judgement of the 'ordinary, reasonable person'.
263. For example, a Gallup poll conducted in the UK, US and Canada found 77, 43 and 75 per cent in favour of UBI respectively, but the question was loaded by framing the policy as 'a way to help people who lose their jobs because of advances in artificial intelligence'. A similar poll reported by *The Hill* presented UBI as 'a proposal to help Americans whose jobs are threatened by automation'. Of course, most working people can see themselves as potential beneficiaries of such a policy. If the questions had framed UBI as 'a way to help college graduates who can't find a job they like the look of' or 'some help for people who like to work only in the afternoon' I'm fairly

confident that the support would have been considerably thinner. Obviously any question about Universal Basic Income should come without a hint of non-universality. More carefully conducted research generally reveals considerable scepticism about UBI, and genuine concerns about detailed mechanisms, even among potential advocates. https://news.gallup.com/poll/267143/universal-basic-income-favored-canada-not.aspx https://thehill.com/hilltv/what-americas-thinking/512099-poll-majority-of-voters-now-say-the-government-should-have-a

264. For example https://www.thersa.org/globalassets/_foundation/new-site-blocks-and-images/reports/2020/10/the-rsa-a-popular-basic-income.pdf
265. https://www.kingsfund.org.uk/projects/nhs-in-a-nutshell/nhs-workforce https://www.ons.gov.uk/peoplepopulationandcommunity/healthandsocialcare/healthcaresystem/bulletins/ukhealthaccounts/2018
266. MEEK, J. *Private Island – why Britain now belongs to someone else*. Verso, 2015. p192.
267. CHRISTOPHERS, B. (2018) p2.
268. PIKETTY, T. (2020) p1009.
269. Of course, worker-owned co-operatives could remain entirely unaccountable to the public and act as a form of private enterprise. It clearly makes sense, though, to encourage a model of co-op that receives public support (whether direct financing or public contract eligibility or something else) in return for meeting certain criteria, including a measure of public accountability.
270. A concern for socialists when considering a mixed economy is that the private sector may eventually produce a wealthy bourgeois class, who would gain disproportionate political power and plunge us back into capitalism. The programmes detailed here should

provide economic mechanisms capable of preventing this outcome, but it may also be necessary to eventually add political measures to reinforce this position. Such measures would have to emerge over time.

271. Public ownership, as we noted earlier, is not limited to state ownership. Local government and worker-owner co-operatives are obvious alternatives, and there's every reason to think that more alternatives will emerge over time.
272. Some argue that our system is not broken, but was designed to be an undemocratic servant of the wealthy. There is some truth to this, but there is also truth in the idea that some of the most dysfunctional aspects of our system arose accidentally, rather than by design. Our appalling electoral system, for example, evolved over centuries and calls for universal suffrage were not accompanied by calls for proportionality because it's only when people see our system in action that they realise how undemocratic it is.
273. Constituency electorates in the UK vary by a factor of five from 21,106 to 113,021.
274. In 1951, for example, Labour received a quarter of a million more votes than the Conservatives, but the Conservatives won a majority in Parliament and formed the government.
275. https://web.archive.org/web/20151031082741/ http://www.hansardsociety.org.uk/wp-content/uploads/ 2012/10/Commission-on-Electoral-Reform-1976.pdf
276. This system also provides us with a number of MPs in addition to the one-per-constituency we are used to under the current system. These 'spare' MPs can be used to improve the representational role of MPs. It might be that a spare MP on the government benches assists with local duties for the otherwise engaged PM, or other cabinet members, whose constituents get a pretty raw deal in terms of local representation under the

present system. Opposition parties could make similar arrangements to cover constituency duties for their senior MPs. Other MPs might be used to provide an additional layer of representation for voters saddled with an MP of a different political persuasion to their own. A spare Labour MP might give Labour voters in the Home Counties, for example, a sympathetic representative – *in addition to* the endless stream of Tory MPs who are part of the furniture at the local golf and country club. Similarly, a spare Tory MP might be assigned to represent the dozen or so people in Liverpool who still buy *The Sun* and are consequently too embarrassed to take their grievances to their sitting Labour MP.

277. https://labourlist.org/2020/06/ministers-ignorance-of-marmot-review-is-shameful-says-ashworth/
278. Thomas Piketty discusses how such a scheme might work in PIKETTY, T. (2020) p1017.
279. UETRICHT, M. and DAY, M. *Bigger Than Bernie: How We Go from the Sanders Campaign to Democratic Socialism*. Verso 2020.
280. SUNKARA, B. *The Socialist Manifesto – The Case for Radical Politics in an Era of Extreme Inequality*. Verso, 2019.
281. GILBERT, J. *Twenty-First Century Socialism*. Polity, 2020.

Works Cited

ADAMS, D. *The Hitchhikers Guide to the Galaxy Original Radio Scripts*. Harmony Books, 1985

ALBERT, M. and HAHNEL, R. *The Political Economy of Participatory Economics*. Princeton University Press, 1991

ANDERSON, P. *Passages from Antiquity to Feudalism*. Verso, 2013

ASHFORD, N. *Principles for a Free Society* (2nd edition). Blomberg & Janson, 2003

ATKINSON, A, *Inequality: What can be done?* Harvard University Press, 2018

BASTANI, A. *Fully Automated Luxury Communism*. Verso, 2018

BERLIN, I. *Four Essays on Liberty*. Oxford University Press, 1969

BRYNJOLFSSON, E. and McAFEE, A. The Second Machine Age – Work, Progress, and Prosperity in a Time of Brilliant Technologies. W. W. Norton, 2016

BURKE, E. *Reflections on the Revolution in France* (1790). Jonathan Bennett, 2017. (See https://www.earlymoderntexts.com/assets/pdfs/burke1790part1.pdf)

CHRISTOPHERS, B. *The New Enclosure – The Appropriation of Public Land in Neoliberal Britain*. Verso, 2019.

CLARK, J.C.D. *English Society 1688-1832*. Cambridge University Press, 1985

COHEN, G.A. *Karl Marx's Theory of History – A Defence*. Princeton University Press, 1976

COHEN, G.A. Functional Explanation: Reply to Elster. *Political Studies* Vol.XXVIII, No.1. 1980

COHEN, G.A. *Why Not Socialism?* Princeton University Press, 2009

COHEN, G.A. *On the Currency of Egalitarian Justice and Other Essays in Political Philosophy*. Princeton, 2011

COLLEY, T. ,GRANELLI, F. and ALTHUIS, J. Disinformation's Societal Impact: Britain, Covid, And Beyond. *Defence*

Strategic Communications (NATO), Volume 8, Spring 2020

COWLING, M. (ed.) *The Communist Manifesto: New Interpretations*. Edinburgh University Press, 1998

DEATON, A. *The Great Escape – health, wealth, and the origins of inequality*. Princeton University Press, 2013

EYSENCK, H.J. *Sense and Nonsense in Psychology. Penguin, 1956*

FERGUSON, L.W.*'The Stability of the Primary Social Attitudes: I. Religionism and Humanitarianism'. Journal of Psychology*. 1941, *12*

FISHER, M. *Capitalist Realism – is there no alternative?* Zero Books, 2009.

FORD, M. *Rise of the Robots –Technology and the Threat of a Jobless Future*. Basic Books, 2015.

FRANCE, A. *Le Lys Rouge*. Calmann-Lévy, 1894.

FRANKFURT, H. Equality as a Moral Ideal. *Ethics Vol. 98, No. 1* Oct., 1987. pp. 21-43

FRIEDMAN, M. *Capitalism and Freedom*. University Of Chicago Press, 1982

GALBRAITH, James.K. *Inequality and Instability. A Study of the World Economy Just Before the Great Crisis*. Oxford University Press, 2012

GALBRAITH, J.K. 'Let us begin: An invitation to action on poverty' in *Harper's* March, 1964

GALLMAN, R. E. 'Self-Sufficiency in the Cotton Economy of the Antebellum South' in PARKER, W.N. (ed.), *The Structure of the Cotton Economy of the Antebellum South*. Agricultural History Society, 1970

GILBERT, J. *Twenty-First Century Socialism. Polity*, 2020

GOLDTHORPE, J.H. et al. The Affluent Worker and the Thesis of Embourgeoisement: Some Preliminary Research Findings, *Sociology*. 1967

GOLDTHORPE, J.H. et al. *The Affluent Worker in the Class Structure*. Cambridge University Press, 1969

GRAEBER, D. *Bullshit Jobs – the rise of pointless work and what we can do about it*. Penguin, 2018

GRAY, A. *The Socialist Tradition*. Harper & Row, 1968

HAHNEL, R. and WRIGHT, E.O. *Alternatives to Capitalism*. Verso, 2014

HAYEK, F.A. *The Road to Serfdom*. Routledge, 2001

HAYEK, F.A. *The Constitution of Liberty*. Chicago University Press, 1960

HILTON, R.H. (ed.) *The Transition from Feudalism to Capitalism*. New Left Books, 1976

HOBSBAWM, E. *How to Change the World: Tales of Marx and Marxism*. Abacus, 2012

HOBSBAWM, E. and RUDE, G. *Captain Swing*. Phoenix, 2001

HODGES, D. The Intermediate Classes in Marxian Theory. *Social Research*, 23, 1961

HUDSON, M. *Killing the Host: How financial parasites and debt bondage destroy the global economy*. Islet, 2015.

KAPLAN, J. *Humans Need Not Apply: A Guide to Wealth and Work in the Age of Artificial Intelligence*. Yale University Press, 2015

KAYE, H.J. *The British Marxist Historians*. Polity Press, 1984

KELTON, S. *The Deficit Myth*. John Murray, 2020

KLEBNIKOV,P.G. *Agricultural Development in Russia, 1906-17: Land Reform, Social Agronomy and Cooperation*. 1991. p 352 (PhD Dissertation, at http://etheses.lse.ac.uk/1141/1/U048311.pdf)

LERNER, A.P. 'Functional Finance and the Federal Debt' in *Social Research*, Vol. 10, No. 1 (Feb. 1943)

LERNER, A.P. *The Economic Steering Wheel*. NYU Press, 1983

LOCKE, J. *Second Treatise on Government and A Letter Concerning Toleration*. Oxford, 2016

LOCKWOOD, D. The 'New Working Class' in *European Journal of Sociology*. Vol. 1, No. 2, (1960), pp. 248-259

MARX,K. *Capital I*. Lawrence & Wishart, 1954

MARX, K. *Capital III*. Lawrence & Wishart, 1959

MARX, K *and* ENGELS, F. *Collected Works*. Lawrence & Wishart, 1975 (Volumes 5, 6, 20, 24, 34, 38)

McCLELLAND, P. and ZECKHAUSER, R. *Demographic Dimensions of the New Republic*. Cambridge University Press, 1982

MEEK, J. *Private Island – why Britain now belongs to someone else*. Verso, 2015

MEISKINS WOOD, E. *The Origins of Capitalism*. Verso 1999

MEISKINS WOOD, E. *Liberty and Property*. Verso 2012

MITCHELL, B.P. *Eight Ways to Run the Country: a new and revealing look at left and right*. Greenwood, 2007

MITCHELL, B.R. *International Historical Statistics – Europe 1750-1988* (3rd ed.) Macmillan, 1992

MITCHELL, W.F. and WRAY, L. R. *Full Employment through a Job Guarantee: A Response to the Critics*, 2005. Available at SSRN: https://ssrn.com/abstract=1010149

MORE, T. *Utopia*. Cassell & Company, 1901

MURO, M. et al. *What Jobs are Affected by AI?* Brookings Institution, 2019 https://www.brookings.edu/research/what-jobs-are-affected-by-ai-better-paid-better-educated-workers-face-the-most-exposure/

NAGEL,T. *Equality and Partiality*. Oxford University Press, 1991

NAGEL, T. and MURPHY, L. *The Myth of Ownership: Taxes and Justice*. Oxford University Press, 2004

NOZICK, R. *Anarchy, State and Utopia*. Basil Blackwell, 1974

ORWELL, G. *Animal Farm*. Penguin, 2008

OVERTON, M. *Agricultural Revolution in England – The Transformation of the Agrarian Economy 1500-1850*. Cambridge University Press, 1996

PAINE, T. *Rights of Man, Common Sense and Other Political Writings*. Oxford University Press, 1995

PAXTON, S. *Unlearning Marx – Why the Soviet failure was a triumph for Marx*. Zero Books, 2021

PEEL, F. *The Risings of the Luddites*. Nabu Press, 2011

PETTIFOR, A. *The Production of Money – How to break the power of bankers*. Verso, 2017.

PIKETTY, T. *Capital in the Twenty-First Century*. Harvard University Press, 2017

PIKETTY, T. *Capital and Ideology*. Harvard University Press, 2020

PLEKHANOV, G.V. *The Development of the Monist View of History*. Moscow, 1972

POLANYI, K.*The Great Transformation – The Political and Economic Origins of Our Time (2nd ed.)* Beacon Press, 2001

PUSHKAREV, S. *The Emergence of Modern Russia 1801-1917*. Pica Pica Press, 1985

RAWLS, J. *A Theory of Justice*. Clarendon, 1971

RAWLS, J. *Justice as Fairness A Restatement*. Harvard University Press, 2001

REICH, R. B. *The System – Who Rigged it, How to Fix it*. Alfred A. Knopf, 2020

ROKEACH, M. *The Nature of Human Values*. Free Press, 1973

ROTHBARD,M. *The Ethics of Liberty*. New York University Press, 2002

ROUSSEAU, J-J. *The Social Contract*. Wordsworth, 1998

RUSSELL, B. *In Praise of Idleness*. Unwin, 1976

SEN, A. *Equality of What?* The Tanner Lecture on Human Values, Stanford University, 1979 http://www.ophi.org.uk/wp-content/uploads/Sen-1979_Equality-of-What.pdf

SHRUBSOLE, G. *Who Owns England – How We Lost Our Land and How to Take it Back*. William Collins, 2019

SMITH, A. *An Inquiry into the Nature and Causes of the Wealth of Nations Books IV-V*. Penguin, 1999

SMITHIN, J. *What is Money?* Routledge, 1999

STIGLITZ, J.E. *The Great Divide*. Penguin, 2015

STIGLITZ, J.E. *The Price of Inequality*. Norton, 2013

STUART, J. (James I and VI) *The Trve Law of Free Monarchies*. 1598

SUNKARA, B. *The Socialist Manifesto – The Case for Radical*

Politics in an Era of Extreme Inequality. Verso, 2019

UETRICHT, M. and DAY, M. *Bigger Than Bernie: How We Go from the Sanders Campaign to Democratic Socialism*. Verso 2020

VONNEGUT, K. *Welcome to the Monkey House.* Harper Collins, 1972

VONNEGUT, K. *Breakfast of Champions*. Grafton, 1974

WEBB, M, *The Impact of Artificial Intelligence on the Labor Market*. 2019 Available at SSRN: https://ssrn.com/abstract=3482150

WILKINSON, R. and PICKETT, K. *The Spirit Level – Why Equality is Better for Everyone*. Penguin, 2010

WINSTANLEY, G. *The Law of Freedom in a Platform*, Benediction Books, 2009

WOODHOUSE, A.S.P *Puritanism and Liberty – Being the Army Debates (1647-49) from the Clarke Manuscripts with Supporting Documents*. University of Chicago Press, 1951

WRAY, L.R. Modern Money in SMITHIN, J. *What is Money?* Routledge, 1999

WRIGHT, G. *The Political Economy of the Cotton South*. W.W. Norton, 1978

WRIGHT, G. *Slavery and Anglo-American Capitalism Revisited.* Tawney Lecture to the Economic History Society, Belfast, 2019. Available online at https://drive.google.com/file/d/1ZLLNGFiwtrjeza5oZwFQRG-J3MQdn1cP/view

CULTURE, SOCIETY & POLITICS

Contemporary culture has eliminated the concept and public figure of the intellectual. A cretinous anti-intellectualism presides, cheer-led by hacks in the pay of multinational corporations who reassure their bored readers that there is no need to rouse themselves from their stupor. Zer0 Books knows that another kind of discourse - intellectual without being academic, popular without being populist - is not only possible: it is already flourishing. Zer0 is convinced that in the unthinking, blandly consensual culture in which we live, critical and engaged theoretical reflection is more important than ever before.

If you have enjoyed this book, why not tell other readers by posting a review on your preferred book site.

You may also wish to subscribe to our Zer0 Books YouTube Channel.

Bestsellers from Zer0 Books include:

Give Them An Argument

Logic for the Left

Ben Burgis

Many serious leftists have learned to distrust talk of logic. This is a serious mistake.

Paperback: 978-1-78904-210-8 ebook: 978-1-78904-211-5

Poor but Sexy

Culture Clashes in Europe East and West

Agata Pyzik

How the East stayed East and the West stayed West.

Paperback: 978-1-78099-394-2 ebook: 978-1-78099-395-9

An Anthropology of Nothing in Particular

Martin Demant Frederiksen

A journey into the social lives of meaninglessness.

Paperback: 978-1-78535-699-5 ebook: 978-1-78535-700-8

In the Dust of This Planet

Horror of Philosophy vol. 1

Eugene Thacker

In the first of a series of three books on the Horror of Philosophy, *In the Dust of This Planet* offers the genre of horror as a way of thinking about the unthinkable.

Paperback: 978-1-84694-676-9 ebook: 978-1-78099-010-1

The End of Oulipo?

An Attempt to Exhaust a Movement

Lauren Elkin, Veronica Esposito

Paperback: 978-1-78099-655-4 ebook: 978-1-78099-656-1

Capitalist Realism

Is There No Alternative?

Mark Fisher

An analysis of the ways in which capitalism has presented itself as the only realistic political-economic system.

Paperback: 978-1-84694-317-1 ebook: 978-1-78099-734-6

Rebel Rebel

Chris O'Leary

David Bowie: every single song. Everything you want to know, everything you didn't know.

Paperback: 978-1-78099-244-0 ebook: 978-1-78099-713-1

Kill All Normies

Angela Nagle

Online culture wars from 4chan and Tumblr to Trump.

Paperback: 978-1-78535-543-1 ebook: 978-1-78535-544-8

Cartographies of the Absolute

Alberto Toscano, Jeff Kinkle

An aesthetics of the economy for the twenty-first century.

Paperback: 978-1-78099-275-4 ebook: 978-1-78279-973-3

Malign Velocities

Accelerationism and Capitalism

Benjamin Noys

Long listed for the Bread and Roses Prize 2015, *Malign Velocities* argues against the need for speed, tracking acceleration as the symptom of the ongoing crises of capitalism.

Paperback: 978-1-78279-300-7 ebook: 978-1-78279-299-4

Meat Market

Female Flesh under Capitalism

Laurie Penny

A feminist dissection of women's bodies as the fleshy fulcrum of capitalist cannibalism, whereby women are both consumers and consumed.

Paperback: 978-1-84694-521-2 ebook: 978-1-84694-782-7

Babbling Corpse

Vaporwave and the Commodification of Ghosts

Grafton Tanner

Paperback: 978-1-78279-759-3 ebook: 978-1-78279-760-9

New Work New Culture

Work we want and a culture that strengthens us

Frithjof Bergmann

A serious alternative for mankind and the planet.

Paperback: 978-1-78904-064-7 ebook: 978-1-78904-065-4

Romeo and Juliet in Palestine

Teaching Under Occupation

Tom Sperlinger

Life in the West Bank, the nature of pedagogy and the role of a university under occupation.

Paperback: 978-1-78279-637-4 ebook: 978-1-78279-636-7

Color, Facture, Art and Design

Iona Singh

This materialist definition of fine-art develops guidelines for architecture, design, cultural-studies and ultimately social change.

Paperback: 978-1-78099-629-5 ebook: 978-1-78099-630-1

Sweetening the Pill

or How We Got Hooked on Hormonal Birth Control

Holly Grigg-Spall

Has contraception liberated or oppressed women? *Sweetening the Pill* breaks the silence on the dark side of hormonal contraception.

Paperback: 978-1-78099-607-3 ebook: 978-1-78099-608-0

Why Are We The Good Guys?

Reclaiming Your Mind from the Delusions of Propaganda

David Cromwell

A provocative challenge to the standard ideology that Western power is a benevolent force in the world.

Paperback: 978-1-78099-365-2 ebook: 978-1-78099-366-9

The Writing on the Wall

On the Decomposition of Capitalism and its Critics

Anselm Jappe, Alastair Hemmens

A new approach to the meaning of social emancipation.

Paperback: 978-1-78535-581-3 ebook: 978-1-78535-582-0

Enjoying It

Candy Crush and Capitalism

Alfie Bown

A study of enjoyment and of the enjoyment of studying. Bown asks what enjoyment says about us and what we say about enjoyment, and why.

Paperback: 978-1-78535-155-6 ebook: 978-1-78535-156-3

Ghosts of My Life

Writings on Depression, Hauntology and Lost Futures

Mark Fisher

Paperback: 978-1-78099-226-6 ebook: 978-1-78279-624-4

Neglected or Misunderstood

The Radical Feminism of Shulamith Firestone

Victoria Margree

An interrogation of issues surrounding gender, biology, sexuality, work and technology, and the ways in which our imaginations continue to be in thrall to ideologies of maternity and the nuclear family.

Paperback: 978-1-78535-539-4 ebook: 978-1-78535-540-0

How to Dismantle the NHS in 10 Easy Steps (Second Edition)

Youssef El-Gingihy

The story of how your NHS was sold off and why you will have to buy private health insurance soon. A new expanded second edition with chapters on junior doctors' strikes and government blueprints for US-style healthcare.

Paperback: 978-1-78904-178-1 ebook: 978-1-78904-179-8

Digesting Recipes

The Art of Culinary Notation

Susannah Worth

A recipe is an instruction, the imperative tone of the expert, but this constraint can offer its own kind of potential. A recipe need not be a domestic trap but might instead offer escape – something to fantasise about or aspire to.

Paperback: 978-1-78279-860-6 ebook: 978-1-78279-859-0

Most titles are published in paperback and as an ebook. Paperbacks are available in traditional bookshops. Both print and ebook formats are available online.

Follow us at:

https://www.facebook.com/ZeroBooks

https://twitter.com/Zer0Books

https://www.instagram.com/zero.books